D0175383

Every woman should know that she is loved and valued simply for being who she is. In *Beautiful Lies* Jennifer reveals the lies that so many women believe. She tells her story honestly and compellingly and then offers practical hope for all of us as we seek to live a life of meaning. This book will help everyone who reads it!

Holly Wagner,
author and founder of *GodChicks* and *Survival Guide for Young Women*

Beautiful Lies is a book every woman should read. Jennifer Strickland weaves the powerful story of her life throughout each chapter while emphasizing transformational truths from God's Word. Her vulnerability, exquisite writing style, and practical take-home applications make this book the ideal choice for personal or for small group use.

Carol Kent,
speaker and author of *Becoming a Woman of Influence*

Jennifer Strickland's story is absolutely compelling. It reads like a novel but it is real life. There isn't a young girl or woman in the universe who would not be enthralled with this message. As a beautiful young model, Jennifer found emptiness and deep sorrowful pain. Yet today she is a wonderful wife and mother who has found true beauty, hope, and restoration. It's a message for this generation.

Jim Burns, PhD,
President of HomeWord and author of *Confident Parenting* and *Teenology*

This is not another "how to" book. This is a personal journey shared by Jennifer. She opens her heart and exposes the pain she experienced while being a successful model. Jennifer puts her modeling experiences on paper in a beautiful, descriptive way. I too went through these same feelings of rejection and being treated like an object and not a person. Sometimes we have to go on an emotional roller coaster to find true love. Come share Jennifer's journey as she discovers what beauty really is. This book will help you to identify the lies and deceptions of the world and help you find the true meaning of beauty, acceptance, and love.

Kim Alexis,
spokesperson and author,
former *Cosmopolitan* and *Sports Illustrated* cover girl

There is a spiritual battle for the minds and hearts of women. It's real and it's raw and it's destroying lives. With transparency and authenticity Jennifer uncovers lies, deception, and distractions that keep women searching for something that will never satisfy. This book is a message of healing truth, spiritual realities, love, and freedom that every woman longs for. Jennifer tackles the tough struggles and issues that women have learned to hide and helps us find hope in our true identity and purpose.

Debbie Stuart,
Church and Leadership Development Director, Women of Faith

I am a big believer that destructive lies are rooted out only by truth. As an eyewitness to the sinister power of lies in the lives of those God loves, Jennifer Strickland offers good news to girls and women who have believed the lie that they're not worth much. *Beautiful Lies* is food for those who hunger for that which really satisfies.

Margot Starbuck,
author of *Unsqueezed*

Beautiful Lies captivated my heart in so many ways! The stories of Jennifer's life brought me from a place of clinging to a place of surrendering. Jennifer reminded me of a better way to live—to move from being a victim who lives in fear to loving myself through God's eyes and living in freedom! If every parent read this book, they would know how to bless their daughters. If every woman read this book, we could move from living in isolation to living in true community.

Pat Cimo,
Family Life Director, Willow Creek Church

Beautiful Lies is a must-read for women today. We are lured and seduced to the lies of magazines in stores, our image in a mirror, and the approval of men—only to leave us haunted by what-ifs. *Beautiful Lies* is a true story of Jen's authentic journey and insight into the traps of the world and the redeeming love and healing that can only come from God, the creator of beauty and our true identity.

Debbie Eaton,
Director of Women's Ministry, Saddleback Church

jennifer
strickland

beautiful Lies

CONCORDIA UNIVERSITY LIBRARY
PORTLAND, OR 97211

HARVEST HOUSE PUBLISHERS
EUGENE, OREGON

Unless otherwise indicated, all Scripture quotations are from the Holy Bible, New International Version®, NIV®. Copyright © 1973, 1978, 1984, 2011, by Biblica, Inc.™ Used by permission of Zondervan. All rights reserved worldwide. www.zondervan.com

Verses marked MSG are taken from The Message. Copyright © by Eugene H. Peterson 1993, 1994, 1995, 1996, 2000, 2001, 2002. Used by permission of NavPress Publishing Group.

Cover by Left Coast Design, Portland, Oregon

Published in association with the literary agency of WordServe Literary Group, Ltd., 10152 S. Knoll Circle, Highlands Ranch, CO 80130

Backcover author photo by Natasha Brown Photography (www.natashabrownphoto.com).

Cover illustration © Shutterstock / jumpingsack

BEAUTIFUL LIES

Copyright © 2013 by Jennifer Strickland
Published by Harvest House Publishers
Eugene, Oregon 97402
www.harvesthousepublishers.com

Library of Congress Cataloging-in-Publication Data
    Strickland, Jennifer.
    Beautiful lies / Jennifer Strickland.
        pages cm
    Includes bibliographical references.
    ISBN 978-0-7369-5624-6 (pbk.)
    ISBN 978-0-7369-5625-3 (eBook)
    1. Christian women—Religious life. 2. Self-esteem in women—Religious aspects—Christianity. I. Title.
    BV4527.S744 2013
    248.8'43—dc23

                                                      2013006542

All rights reserved. No part of this publication may be reproduced, stored in a retrieval system, or transmitted in any form or by any means—electronic, mechanical, digital, photocopy, recording, or any other—except for brief quotations in printed reviews, without the prior permission of the publisher.

Printed in the United States of America

            13 14 15 16 17 18 19 20 21 / VP-JH / 10 9 8 7 6 5 4 3 2 1

For Linda
May the legacy of your unwavering faith,
selfless love, and priceless prayers live on
through these pages.

Acknowledgments

My husband, Shane, is to thank for this book. Sometimes I was so afraid of what might come out should I put pen to paper that I tried to stall the fulfillment of my own dream. Yet Shane relentlessly pointed to the goal as the sunrise on the horizon, not letting me run away for fear I would fail, and believing if I sprinted toward that horizon, my dream would come true. Surely our Father worked through Shane in this; as I hand this book over to you, the sun is dawning a new day in my heart.

Creating something beautiful from mounds of uneven dirt is Shane's parents' expertise. My gratitude goes to his father, Larry, a builder at heart, who continually advises me on how to build a dream from a blank page. Shane's mother, Linda, has believed for this message, sacrificed for it, and guided me with her gentle and quiet spirit—as sweet as the lamb, as sure as the lion.

I am grateful to my parents, George and Jan Porter, who gave me life and who continue to give my dreams life. As Mom says, she will give as long as she lives, and even after she's gone. Mom and Dad, I hope this work will impact lives long beyond our years as well.

To Olivia, our daughter: Thank you for knowing which nights to say quietly from under the covers, "Mommy, you should stay up and write," and which nights to say, "Mommy, sleep." Thank you to our son Zach, who is always comforted to know I am writing in the next room as he drifts into a slumber. For Samuel, the baby of the family—one day you will know your Mommy dreamed and your Daddy believed in her dreams and made sure they happened.

These women were wings, fellow travelers, and a nest to land in: Devi Titus, Leah Springer, Megan Carter, Tracy Levinson, Deana Morgan, and Gayle Novak. Thank you for carrying me toward the sunrise when I couldn't see the way.

I am indebted to the JSM Team: Caris Leidner, for reading, editing, and praying; April Cousens, for roping in the details so I could write; Jan Alexander, for her years of selfless service; Kelly Tookey, for facing the numbers so I didn't have to; Faith Stansky, for her graceful example of real beauty; Wendy Pryne, for the jewelry to match the message; and Rachel Dee Turner, for her myriad of gifts which have propelled this message. Ladies, together, we have poured out our oil.

Thank you finally to Greg Johnson of Wordserve Literary, who keeps believing a former model can actually speak and write, and to the team at Harvest House: Bob Hawkins Jr., LaRae Weikert, Pat Mathis, and Kathleen Kerr, my brilliant editor who helped me craft the stories that have stirred in my soul. You saw my vision and gave it wings.

Contents

Introduction

The phone call came in the late afternoon. We had finished sweeping the house early that morning. Mysteriously, the alarm was blaring incessantly, and no one could turn it off. The new owners said there was a mirror shattered in one of the upstairs rooms, reflective glass in a million pieces scattered all over the floor.

The mirror didn't crash when we were there; Linda cleaned it herself. We left the house completely intact, and the alarm hadn't been set for years. It was a mystery.

Yet I had been shattering masks and crushing mirrors for years, and now, even now, I am exposing their broken pieces for you in these pages: the mirror of man; the bathroom mirror; the mirror of the magazines, the masquerade, and the media. To believe these mirrors declare a woman's beauty, value, and purpose is to believe beautiful lies.

I am familiar with the world which says a woman's reflection is her worth more than I am familiar with any other part of the world. As a young girl, I began modeling, posing for the camera, walking on runways, and appearing in magazines, which launched me into a life that eventually became a beautiful lie. Over time, modeling built me up, but at the peak of my success, the lies shattered me into broken little pieces. An alarm blared in my soul in the middle of the night; and I went in search of beautiful truth.

When I found Truth, I unearthed a beauty that lasts. I left the modeling world, free to take off the masks, knowing that beneath them, we are made for more.

A young girl who begins to believe a lie may never be the same again. The lie begins with trusting in her beauty; it ends with shattering pain. In the modeling industry, which is simply a mirror reflection of the values upheld by the world, we were taught to find our value in the man standing in front of us or the image in the mirror. But the pictures in the magazines were a trick, somehow convincing us that image was supposed to be true to life. In that world, we were taught that shining outside the home was always more important than anything we did within it; and we were taught, as the media reflects, that a woman's worth was in her face, body, and bed. The impact of these lies is tragic.

This book is my offering, my answer, my battle cry. Come with me. Let's look at some mirrors. Let's shatter them. And let's see if there isn't a God who carefully lifts the jewels from the floors of our hearts and forms them into diamonds reflecting his view of real beauty, worth, and purpose.

You are more than what men think; what the mirror reflects; what the magazines tell you. You are more than the mask you wear and the many faces of the media. You are a daughter, a creation, a temple, a light, an ambassador, called into a dark world as a living stone, reflecting the face of God who made you.

Lies can be pretty, but Truth is beautiful. As hard as it is to look square in the eye, truth does free us. And it doesn't wrinkle. Living within you, it grows more brilliant, evermore.

Welcome to this journey. I invite you into my heart, and yours.

Masks can be beautiful on the surface,
but steal the heart of joy;
yet stunning is the one who isn't afraid of her secrets.

1   The First Lie:

You Are What Man Thinks of You

I used to think man could measure my value, but
now I see no man is a reflection of me.

In Search of a King

Gazing into the hazel wells of his eyes, I dive into the spark of light embedded there. The light funnels me into another world, basked in beauty. The warm wind rushes through my hair; I swim and fly at the same time.

Here on earth, my husband kisses me, but in my mind, we are on the edge of the thicket, where the meadow meets the woods. The whole world around us is alive with wonder. The floor of the thicket bends beneath our footsteps; perfect peace is ours. Union is our Master.

He is man; I am woman; stitched together by God.

Someday, there will be no pain, no division, no heartbreak, and no tears.

Someday, there will only be the fullness of joy.

What is it about the fairy tales that make them such a beautiful lie?

Before the Disney princess meets the prince, she is just a common girl. Desperate, lonely, lost, and poor, she has little chance to escape the ruthless world. But once the prince on the white horse gallops into the scene, the view shifts.

In the prince, there is safety from the sorrow of her upbringing. Somehow all the broken places are healed—the mother who didn't love her, the father who wasn't there, the siblings who envied and scorned her, the poverty that humbled her. In the prince, she is healed and set free. He is a new day, the dawn of her dark night.

The prince does what no one before him can do: he slays the enemy who so hungered to devour her and rob her of her rightful place in the kingdom. Willing even to die for her, the prince becomes her salvation. He descends on bended knee to ask her hand, rescuing her from a life of lonely torment. The moment she agrees to marriage, she transforms from a lowly girl dressed in rags to a beloved princess, gowned and crowned.

The future is now bright for her. She's beautiful, she's precious, she's chosen, she's redeemed. Never again will she worry about her former sorrow or question her value or destiny. All of that is settled in the prince.

As a young woman, I believed the redemption of the fairy tales. I wanted the prince and the castle and the crown. So in high school and college, I put my hope in the future. If the future appeared clothed as a boy and promised me love, I handed him my heart, and with that went my identity and value.

But the boy kept taking my heart and crushing it. One after another blundered down the slippery slope of drugs and alcohol, falling cracked and bleeding at the bottom of his own well. From that place of darkness, again and again, I could not raise him. When you are young, you do not realize what the world can do to a boy, or what a boy can do to himself. I could not fix the problems they had with substance abuse, depression, school, money, and more. Although I tried to throw a rope, they had neither the hope nor the faith to grab it, and I certainly had no muscle to raise them.

Watching their souls wither, my heart withered too. They were supposed to save me! They were supposed to throw the rope! They couldn't promise me anything, and if they did make a promise, they didn't keep it. I wanted love to prevail, but I couldn't make it.

My heart torn, my soul bore the mark of loss. I became disenchanted and lost, wishing to wander the world in hopes of finding something else to fill me. My soul craved unfailing love, but I decided that if boys would fail me, I would conquer the world on my own. I would slay my own dragons. I would find my own castle, and I would build my own dreams.

For me, these wishes were potential realities. I often had a plane ticket to take me away, an escape route the average princess might appreciate.

My journey as a fashion model began when I was eight. My mother enrolled me in a Cinderella class at a local charm school, hoping to help me with my coordination and give me some grace. I was quite tall and inept at sports, but modeling was not hard for me. Time and again, I won "Miss Photogenic" in pageants, and when I graduated from the charm school, my tall, sleek, elegant teacher named me "Most Potential Model."

Throughout high school, my mother and I heard that if we really wanted to know if I could make it in the business, I needed to meet Nina Blanchard, the legendary empress of the West Coast modeling world.

So, at six feet tall and seventeen years old, with blonde locks falling to the middle of my back, I strutted into her Hollywood office wearing high heels and a little black dress, my mother fading into the background.

I'll never forget the way Nina looked up from her spectacles, her judicious eyes scanning me from top to bottom.

"Let me see her pictures," she whispered out of half of her mouth, her deep, scratchy voice commanding the man to her right. Her gaze stayed fixed on me.

I leaned on one heel, then the other.

The man's name was Mack. He had a pocked face and a joker's grin. Polite and professional, he handed Nina my photos and asked us to wait while she examined them with a loupe on a light box.

Windows lined the expansive floor of their offices; the colorful lights of Hollywood Boulevard gleamed behind them. Nina and Mack whispered about me.

Finally he ushered us into her private lair. Mom and I sat down opposite her, a grand mahogany desk between us. Throughout the entire interview she left her thin smoldering cigarette propped in a tray piled with ashes. I tried not to be distracted by the stinging sensation in my nose, the glamorous view of Hollywood's jeweled lights, and the knowledge that this fiery red-haired woman possessed the power to either catapult my dreams to the moon or dash them against the rocks.

Leaning forward, cinching her wrinkled brow, and peering with emerald eyes, Nina spoke to my mother: "She has potential. We want to sign her."

With her veined hands and red porcelain nails, she slid a contract across the desk.

This was the continuation of my first beautiful lie: if a man—or woman—thinks I'm pretty, I am. If he or she thinks I have potential, I do. If they want me, I'm worth wanting.

Nina named me the "Face of the Nineties." She sent me to the offices of L'Oréal, Oil of Olay, Eddie Bauer, and Jordache. She got me in *Glamour, Seventeen, Cosmopolitan,* and *Vogue*. She introduced me to Steven Spielberg, Eileen Ford, Giorgio Armani, and Patrick Demarchelier, the favored photographer of Princess Diana.

Nina was my fairy godmother, and by my first year in college, I could perform a disappearing act at will, a convenient setup for a brokenhearted girl. I could run away on a plane or a train, I could hide behind a mask, I could take a picture and smile.

Upon graduating high school, I moved to Europe on Nina's direction. The money and travel were great, but when the summer ended I returned to LA. While other models forsook school to pursue the fleeting fame of modeling, I didn't. Nina even turned down a potential stint for *Sports Illustrated* for me, insisting I stay in college. For the next four years, I maintained a scholarship and majored in broadcast journalism; deep down, I wanted to speak and write.

But I was also one of those girls in the pictures—the ones you see in shop windows, magazines, and on TV. As soon as classes ended in the summer I flew to Europe. There, the local agency would direct me to buy street and metro maps, hand me an address to my new apartment, and have me write down a list of interviews.

Although I lived with other models, I spent most days alone. I'd go from streets to subway stations to buses to trams to hotels to office buildings to sets, touching up makeup in between interviews, touching base at the agency, allowing makeup artists and hair stylists to make me look like a different person every day.

Because I was so young the lifestyle appeared harmless. My parents, who knew very little about the sordid side of the business, were in great support of my modeling career. Everyone from home cheered me on. They all saw modeling as an opportunity to see the world and make money doing it.

So plane tickets arrived on my doorstep like gifts from my fairy godmother, and off I went.

In seasons and short trips, I lived in Los Angeles, Hamburg, Paris, Athens, and Sydney. After college, I signed with Ford Models New York and almost moved there. But in a twist of fate, I interviewed with an agent from Milan who invited me to come to Italy instead.

At 21, I sat in a corner of my Hollywood agency as an Italian man sat across from me. He had curly blond hair, and with his curious accent he dangled before me the allure of travel, fame, and the promise of a beautiful life in Italy.

My mouth watered; it sounded too sweet. I bit into that gloriously shiny red apple with everything I had. I wanted all our world had to offer.

During my plane ride to Milan, I studied Italian and jotted down translations in my diary, repeating Italian sayings like mantras. *Chi cerca trova*—"He who searches, finds."

"Chi cerca trova…Chi cerca trova…" I would repeat, looking out the plane window at the limitless horizon.

With college behind me and my little Italian phrasebook in hand, I thought myself well-armed. Without school as an anchor grounding me in the States, I didn't have to return home. I held in my hand a passport which could take me from place to place for as long as I wanted.

The agent who had summoned me to Italy convinced me the runway would open the door to success. So prior to arriving I did everything I could to measure up to the standards of the European market: I tanned, fasted, sweat, dieted, ran, did yoga, ran some more, fasted some more, took vitamins and fat burners galore, ran, straightened my hair, ran, bought new clothes, worked out some more, ran some more, fasted some more, took some more fat burners, packed my bags, and practiced my Italian.

But no matter how much you make over your outside, the heart is still marred beneath the surface.

It was on this trip to Italy that I met Damien, a magazine owner and fashion mogul who went on to manage my career. He became a sort of protective father figure to me, or so I thought.

During my first season in Milan I often dined with the agents, clients, and photographers, which was customary for models. These men were typically twice my age or older. Instinctually I knew not to let relations go further than dinner or dancing, but a shadowy line blurs the distinction between obliging the clients as they offer to entertain the models and keeping things on a professional level. I centered these encounters on the hopes that these men were going to advance my career, and I simply desired to experience the "beautiful life" promised me in Italy. What a fool I was to believe that these older men would expect nothing in return. I often found myself in awkward situations where I had to politely or sometimes forcefully let them know I was not interested in them romantically.

But of all of the men I met, Damien was the most interested in me. During my first interview with him, he didn't just look at my pictures. He looked into my eyes. He was in his fifties; I had just turned 22. In an industry where very few recognized the soul of a girl, it seemed like he could see straight into mine.

In the world of fashion, he possessed influence, knowledge, and experience. He knew the photographers, magazine owners, and designers. He could catapult my career with the wave of his hand, which also meant he could bury me with the flick of his thumb.

From the moment I met him, he said that I had a *pace dei sensi,* something difficult to translate, but it is a kind of "sense of peace" or "peace of mind." By this time I was an expert at appearing pulled-together and centered, and he took on my career as his little experiment. He put me on the cover of his magazine. He exposed me to fine dining, "important people," and the haute couture. He treated me like I was his prize.

When I was in a new city where I knew no one and nothing about the way the business worked there, Damien made me feel like he knew everything. With his deceitful accent, he promised he would protect, direct, and promote me—just what a young model wants.

But then the night arrived when he revealed that he really wasn't interested in being a father to me. He wanted more.

Shattered

The water for my tea is boiling so I get up and walk to the kitchen. I fix my tea, and as I return the empty pot to the glass top stove, I linger there for a moment to see the reflection of my face. My friend had warned me before I came to Milan not to enter a man's apartment by myself, but I have ignored his warning.

I sit down close to the fire.

"I have never seen a woman who can come so close to the fire," he says, approaching me from behind.

I have never been this skinny before. I lost all my body fat before coming to Milan, in hopes of getting the runway. I'm cold.

Damien sets down his espresso and wraps his body around my back like a heavy cloak.

Every muscle in my body stiffens in fear and I try to pull away. Forcefully, he pushes my shoulder down to keep me there.

"Damien! No!" I protest, yanking myself away and whisking to the window. "What are you thinking?" I demand. This man is well over twice my age, older than my father.

Without sound, he moves across the room.

"You are afraid to be held," he hisses.

"Leave me alone!" I insist. I whirl around, turning my back to him.

"It really is a pity," he whispers, "Because I just wanted to do you a favor. From the moment I met you I thought to myself, what can I do to get this girl to relax? I wanted to do for you something I have not done for a woman in a very long time. A favor, for you, not for me." His words are venom in my ear.

I am frozen in rage, stuck between him and the window of his high rise apartment. I see a few distant streetlights. They remind me of the lights at Nina's, worlds away. The very first thing she did as my agent was to send me to a photographer's apartment, alone. I was seventeen.

"Why are you so afraid to be held?" he pries.

I turn to face him, seething my disgust through clenched teeth, "I am only afraid to be held by the wrong person!" The truth is, I am terrified to be in this man's presence.

Why have I sunk my teeth into the apple of another man's promises? I want to run. I want to hide. I want to wave a magic wand and disappear. But this is not a fairy tale; this is my life, and I can't get away from it.

Damien is an adept predator. At first he earned my trust. He befriended me. He fed me fine Italian food and wine. He showed me the kingdoms of the world and offered me the runways of Paris. All the while, he must have planned to go in for the kill when I was conveniently right before him, unaware as Snow White who was hunting me. What I should have done—and what I tell other women and girls—is to never allow myself to be alone with a man, and to run far and fast should one attempt to compromise me.

How is it that a girl in her early twenties can honestly believe a man in his late fifties simply enjoys her company? How is it that a college-educated woman can be under this kind of spell?

I begin to tell him I don't want what he wants; I want love. I believe in the prince. I just haven't met him yet, but I know he exists.

"You should give up on love," he says, exhausted. "I don't believe in it anymore."

But I do, and I'm not going to give up believing.

"I am destined for misery," he drones. Why is it that I haven't let this man touch me but I feel soiled in his presence? I fear his misery will be transferred to me.

Suddenly we are cut off by the most wicked explosion I've ever heard. Fire combusts from the kitchen and bursts into the living room where we stand. Flames and shards of glass explode from the kitchen.

He runs screaming, blaming me. You left the gas on!" In a blur he rushes into the fire, cursing and filling buckets of water, frantically pouring them over the flames that are leaping like happy demons.

I am crying and screaming and crawling on the floor trying to sweep up the hot glass. "I'm so sorry, I'm so sorry, but I didn't..."

"Watch out! You are going to get cut!" He is throwing water on the fire and lashing me with hot curses: "Stupid girl! How are you so stupid?"

I say, "My God, my God…"

"No!" he screams. "You'd better thank God that he spared your precious face because it was nearly destroyed! I cannot imagine how deformed you would be!"

When I finally get out of there, fear is running through me like an electric current but I don't know how long it will be until it stops. Shamed and confused, I walk back to my apartment in the dark, shadowed, Milanese streets.

"I never die," Damien had moaned when I was at the door, saying he regretted he had not been standing in the kitchen when it blew. "I have brushed death a thousand times but I never die."

A few weeks later, the agency has scheduled a photo shoot for me at Damien's studio, and they say I have to be there.

When I show up, my skin is broken out. I have been living in Milan for about six months now and my career is moving at the pace of a speeding train. I have been doing the runway, sliding down the steep slope of anorexia. I have no other option of entry for that stage—I have to starve myself.

Now, the anxiety, the fear, the loneliness, and the drugs have all shown up on my skin.

I'm feeling more and more like I want to leave the modeling industry. I can't measure up. I am exhausted from men telling me I should get some sun or get lip injections or take better care of my skin or straighten my hair or wear different shoes or walk this way or that way or gain some weight or lose some. I feel like no matter how hard I try, I always fall short.

The makeup artist is working on my face when Damien comes up

and stands behind me. When I see his reflection in the mirror, my stom-
ach turns. Once, he was like a wing of protection. Now he's a predator.

He analyzes my acne in the mirror. "What is wrong with you?" he
demands, pointing out the imperfections on my face.

Inside, I shrink. I feel like I have a deformity and someone's shed a
spotlight on it, and everyone is pointing at me and laughing.

His son is the photographer, a strange troll-like person in his early
twenties. I do the best I can on the shoot, but inside I'm screaming to be
let loose, to be free of their analysis.

At one time the camera was my friend; now it is a foe. My soul is
literally becoming ill from being painted up, judged, praised, scolded,
examined, and pursued by men. I need a break. I need to breathe…
somewhere without makeup and cameras.

That weekend I choose to get away from it all by staying in a hos-
tel out of town. Under the guise of protection, Damien sends his son "to
make sure nothing happens to me." But that evil troll creeps into my
room in the night and takes what is mine to give.

I was so dead inside. I believed the lie that I was as disposable as the
way they treated me. I believed the lie that I was as worthless as the way
they made me feel. I believed the lie that I was what man said I was. If
I had life to do over again, they would have been the ones shattered and
not me. But I carried the broken pieces inside my heart for years to come.

The fairy tales were a lie. Boys fall, men steal from you, fathers fail,
and kings betray. I was soon to find out, however, that God protects, God
saves, God redeems, and God heals.

When I returned to Milan, Damien discovered what happened
with his son and discarded me. His "love" turned to hatred. He let
me know my *pace dei sensi* had left me. I was just a stupid American
girl with a pretty face, and that was all.

At first I was his prized possession; his little discovery, his corsage, his peach. Now, I was breaking out and anorexic and foolish and broken, and he wanted nothing to do with me.

"I don't need you in my life," he growled at me the last time I saw him. Reaching out to touch me, he pressed his thumb hard into the cystic pimple that flared on the side of my mouth and laughed wickedly at me.

I hurried away from him, running through the rain, my head down so he couldn't see my tears.

Soon afterward, I began to have wicked headaches and blurred eyesight. The acne began to take over my face—a death sentence for a model's career. In search of pleasing my other king, Giorgio Armani, my body became dangerously skeletal. My eyes became sunken and hollow; I no longer looked like the young girl who started out full of life. Darkness clouded my heart and soul.

The word for model in French is *le mannequin,* and that's what we were to most of the men—mannequins upon which they could hang the clothes; mannequins they could position however they wanted; mannequins they could take apart and discard when a new model came to town. Plastic, things to be bought, sold, traded, trashed, and dumped when they were done with us.

Since everyone was telling me I was too thin, I tried to eat heartily for a week or two, even stuffing my face to gain weight. But when I showed up for the spring shows, Armani could feel the extra half inch around my waist. He sent me off the stage. The stylist removed my clothes and left me wondering what just happened, standing alone in the massive dressing room, until someone finally came over and told me they were "finished" with me.

I went back to the agency, and the men there were clearly upset with me. I had been cancelled for the Armani shows, and the rest of my jobs that month were cancelled too.

"You look sick!" my booker said to me across the room in front of everyone. "You are as pale as mozzarella!" Then he turned to another girl, some new, fresh-faced girl who had just come to town, and started lavishing her with praise and attention.

I had allowed man to be my mirror, and in the reflection of that mirror all I saw was a twisted vision of my value: I was only as good as I looked that day. I was only as good as they said I was. One day beautiful, the next not. One day wanted, the next no more.

When I first started modeling, Nina was my mirror. For years and years, the praise of the photographers was my stamp of approval. But now, because of Damien and Armani, because of all the photographers and agents who held their magnifying glass up to me to analyze my appearance, I no longer saw anything good in myself. I only saw what was wrong, what was *not* right about me. The way they saw me became the way I saw myself. These men—the ones who held the measuring tape around my waist, the makeup brush to my eyes, the light meter against my cheek, the ticket to my career—became my source of validation. It was they who measured my beauty, who asked, Is she a high-priced commodity or is she just average? What do you think she is *worth*?

One day you're worth a lot; the next you're worth nothing. Humans can become poisonous prisms, distorting lenses that misshape our value. When we give them the power, they can completely change the way we see ourselves and the way we see the world.

But humans can also act as crystallizing lenses for us, realigning our gaze to the one mirror that never lies.

Chi Cerca Trova

It seemed like there were churches around every bend in Italy. On my way to castings, I would stop on the sidewalks and crane my head up to admire the gargantuan structures. Sometimes as I would look up I would whisper my mantra: *Chi cerca trova.*

He who searches will find.

When I first arrived in Milan, I went into one of the more

intimate churches around the corner from my apartment. Out of curiosity, I copied the aged Italian women: they would drop a coin in the offering box, light a tea candle, bend to one knee, pray, and rise, signing the image of the cross. I did the same thing one morning, and said a prayer for my success there.

Not long afterward, I did have success…as the world defines it. I began working nearly every day, while many of the models were struggling to find work. Lots of precious girls from all corners of the world sought affirmation from men in the business, and rarely received it. I watched their roller coaster rides firsthand, not even realizing I was on the same ride.

Ultimately I wanted love—what we all want—so when the roller coaster of approval and rejection bottomed me out, I began to pray for love instead.

Eager to leave the darkness I found in Milan, I planned to move to Munich, where I could make a lot of money doing catalogue work. But I still had a wandering spirit and the desire to see "the beauty of Italy." So before I left the country, I told my booker to find me a job in Rome. They found me a runway job for one of the gaudiest designers I had ever seen.

For the show, the stylist literally dressed me up like I was a candy cane in stilettos. I struggled not to laugh at how ridiculous the red-and white-striped outfit was, and even on stage, I realized the idiocy of this particular parade. For the grand finale, they sent me down the runway dressed like the bride of Dracula with a ten-foot-long satin and lace train. The extravagant wedding gown arched up in the front to reveal black satin shorts, fishnet stockings, and high heels. The runway was an I-ramp instead of a T, so there was no place for me to turn around at the end. Having not practiced turning in this train that took up half the runway behind me, I stopped for a moment, not knowing how on earth I was going to pivot without tripping over the fabric.

Then an image flashed in my mind: these fancy people, in their tuxedos, diamond tiaras, and fur coats, had beating hearts beneath all those layers. All these people were was only "men." What did I have to fear from them? That I would fall? That they would laugh? Reject me? For one moment, I didn't care.

I grabbed the train in my right hand and whipped it out so that it sailed, all ten feet of it, over their heads. On a coin, I turned and tramped down that runway as everyone gasped and then erupted in applause. I walked off the stage, barely turning my head. I didn't care about the applause anymore; it just didn't satisfy. I couldn't get that crazy outfit off fast enough. I had come to see what was truly beautiful. I had come to see Rome.

I left the hotel before dawn the next morning, clasping my ticket to the Vatican. Standing in St. Peter's Square at the break of daylight was more fulfilling for me than interviewing with Gucci or Versace. I passed by the Swiss guards with their tin-soldier outfits and went into the church. There, to the right of the entrance, was Michaelangelo's *Pieta,* his only signed work: a sculpture of Mary, the mother of Christ, the fallen body of her son collapsed in the massive folds of her robe. In her face I saw the real *pace dei sensi,* the kind of peace which great suffering cannot steal. In her face, I saw beauty—not beauty that is found in magazines. Real beauty, which comes from a life of faith.

As I walked through the seemingly endless hallways of the Vatican museum, I felt like I was on a timeless journey, like the marble floor was moving my feet ahead while a movie played on fast-forward in my mind: image after image, painting after painting, sculpture after sculpture, mile after mile, on all sides I saw *God. Man. Angels. Demons. Sinners. Beggars. Prostitutes. Prophets.* And most of all, *Jesus.*

When I got to the Sistine Chapel, I couldn't imagine there could be more. But there was so much more: cherubim, angels draped in ribbons of purple and gold. Creation, God reaching out and touching the hand of man. Eve, the serpent. The Fall in all its great pain.

I poked my head in other churches in Rome, touching the pews, noticing the people who went through those open doors to pray at all hours of the day and night.

En route back to Milan, I stopped in Siena, a little Tuscan hill town outside of Rome. There, on a bus, I met a girl who saw the city with me the next day. We sat in the square and with simple clarity, she told me I needed Christ in my life. This girl looked me square in the eye, and with her calm, serene voice, told me about Jesus and the Holy Spirit.

"I pray," I said.

"To whom?" she asked, a question I could not answer. In kind, compassionate words, she suggested I pray in the name of Jesus and read the Bible. I just took her advice and tucked it in my back pocket, still believing I could forge my own path and fashion my own dreams.

I went on to Munich, where the days and nights were long. In the dead of winter, I trudged on icy sidewalks from appointment to appointment, shivering to the bone, leaning into the wind. On interviews I faked a smile as yet another man and another woman evaluated my face and body in terms of translated profit. Sometimes the makeup artists and photographers would even command me to "look happier" on the set.

My spirit began clanking its empty cup on the prison cell of my body and I began to turn against my own self. Smoking too much, drinking too much, binging one day and starving the next, I would stay in my bed for long hours while voices ripped at my self-worth, blasting messages through my brain. I wasn't good enough, beautiful enough, perfect enough. No one loved me, no one saw me, no one knew me, there was no way out. The voices circled through my head like a merry-go-round on high.

One night it got to be too much for me. In a moment of quiet, calculated desperation, I attempted to drown myself in the bathtub. The voices were cheering me on.

My head was underwater. The air was running out and I was starting to panic. Then, through my mind's eye, flashed visions of myself as a child. I was pure, I was beautiful, I was free. I was filled with joy. There was no striving and no pain. I thought of my family and remembered that I was loved.

Sobbing and gasping at the same time, I sucked in water, began to cough, and shot up like a geyser from fertile soil.

"Jennifer, get up." The voice beckons. It comes from the window and I sit straight up. I've been lying under layers of blankets for so many hours. My head is throbbing. What time is it? What day is it?

Light streams through the snow-laden glass of the window, casting rainbows on the floor.

Who was that? I could have sworn I heard my name.

I lie back down to keep warm but I'm shivering, freezing. I squeeze my eyes shut and try to go back to sleep. I just want to stay here under the covers.

"Jennifer, get up."

I sit straight up this time; I stand up.

I go into the bathroom and wash my face, trying to not look at the tub. I get dressed. I ignore the flashing light on the answering machine. I know it's my agency telling me about some stupid appointment. I don't want to go. I have been to hundreds of stupid appointments, and I'm not answering that light today.

I take the metro to a park and stay there all day. The Danube rushes through it like an ice blue ribbon weaving through an emerald land-scape. There is a giant stone gazebo perched on a hilltop where people gather in the evenings to watch the sunset, play music, have a picnic, hold hands and talk. I envy the lovers, but more so the friends. I envy the food they eat. I envy their companionship. I envy their smiles, especially their laughter.

I choose a seat at the base of one of the pillars in the gazebo so I can hear some music. This man behind me is singing and strumming his guitar, his voice high and sweet. I turn to look at him and he reaches down into an old cardboard box of books and hands me a German New Testament.

The cover of it is sapphire, and the words are engraved in gold. I take it in my hands.

He and his friends hardly speak any English. They are so kind that when they realize I am alone in the park, they offer to walk me out.

Right when we are nearing the edge of the darkened wood, these strangers stop and pray for me. It is the oddest thing to hear them saying my name in German.

They ask me if I would like to go to church with them that Friday night. I don't feel that anyone else on the continent cares about my well-being, so I go.

Friday comes and the falling snow speckles the night with wonder. They pick me up and drive me to a small brick church on the outskirts of town. When I see it from the car, the windows are all lit up. It's like a glowing topaz stone embedded in the cotton snowdrifts.

When they open the door for me warm air surges out, climbs inside of my coat, and cuddles me like a heated blanket.

I take it like a hug.

If someone could taste joy, I taste it in that place. It whets my palette and my mouth waters at the sweetness. Children run this way and that; adults are laughing. There are big coats and big hugs and big handshakes that rock my bony frame. Smiles and songs fill the room. And although I recognize not a single word of the sermon, my spirit begins to peek its head up from its watery grave.

I go back to the church the next Friday night. The people there are worlds away from what I see in the world of fashion. They speak to me,

*not at me, and try their best to help me understand. They get me a trans-
lator this time who sits next to me and whispers the sermon in my ear.
Afterward they invite me to eat with them, and when we do, no one eyes
the way I eat or excludes me from a story. They don't seem to notice my
imperfections or the fact that my* pace dei sensi *is gone. They don't look
at my body or measurements, but at my heart. I don't feel like I have to
wear any kind of mask when I am with them.*

*When I have questions about this Jesus they talk about, they just
answer them clean and clear. They explain the gospel to me—that faith
in the blood of Christ gives us forgiveness of sin, heaven, and everything
we need for life—and the third time I go to the church, a girl named
Naomi comes bounding out from the back pews with a book in her
hands, barely able to contain her excitement.*

*"Jenny-fair! Jenny-fair! I have found you an English Bible!" she
exclaims, her face radiant.*

*The worn, thin pages feel good in my hands. I shove it in my pocket
and take it home.*

*Back in my apartment at night, I grow curious about that little book.
Somehow it woos me to itself. I begin to thirst only for it, its fragile pages
tender and delicate.*

*The most striking thing about Jesus to me is that he loves those our
world doesn't. He touches those no one wants to touch and befriends
those the prideful people refuse. The people who are full of sin and pain,
the weak, the broken, the confounded—he loves them all. I feel like I
have been waiting my whole life to meet him, and now that I have, I
want to follow him wherever I go. I keep that little book in my back
pocket and read it on trains, waiting for interviews, and at home at
night.*

*By candlelight I eat up most of the book of Matthew, then pack my
backpack for a weekend away. I take a train to the base of Mount Zugspitze, the highest mountain in Germany, and stay at a little bed and
breakfast to finish reading the last few chapters. In my rented room, I sit
at a tiny desk and look out a window at the descending snow. Snuggled*

in a blanket wrapped from my shoulders to my toes, I read the story of the end of Jesus's life.

In the pages of that Word, I discover a man who loves me despite the ways I fall short of man's expectations. I discover a man who accepts me just as I am. A man who offers me freedom from the slavery of my life. A king who will never leave me or forsake me.

I fall so in love with him.

On a white blanket of snow on Mount Zugspitze, I lie down on the ground and open up my heart to Jesus. I know nothing about Scripture or theology or denominations or church. I just know I have found the one my soul loves, and that he is my only hope. There in the snow, I die to the lies of my old life, and when I get up, before me there is a new beginning. I am resuscitated and new.

After fifteen years in the modeling industry, I pack my bags and leave. I don't need to explain to anyone why I am leaving. The people from the church translate to my German agency that I am no longer modeling and ask them to tell the rest of the agencies for me. I am finished.

I leave an entire world behind that says, You are what I say you are. You do what I say you do. And I am done with you when I'm done with you.

This time it is my turn to speak. I say, This is not beautiful to me, and I am leaving in search of what is.

He Who Searches, Finds

In the coming years I fell deeper and deeper in love with my King. When man lied, God told me the truth. When man tried to lure me back to my old ways, God told me to walk away. When man tried to bind me with his rules, God set me free to take his path. When man turned his back on me, God opened his arms.

The things that I couldn't explain I poured out in hungry prayers. Page after page of my diaries, book after book, became filled with prayers, yearnings, questions…and in return came answers through his Word and Spirit. My diaries became a chronicle of our conversations. I asked, hungry to know, and he answered with sips of wisdom, morsels of truth, a feast of faith.

But as is natural, I longed for a man.

Shane came at just the right time, about four years after I left modeling. He was strapping, handsome, strong, funny, faithful, ambitious, and had seen far greater depths than I. In his late teens, he had wandered away from his family and faith, traveling for years in search of what would satisfy. Once he landed at the bottom of his mud-lined and slippery pit, he decided that God and family were the answer to his questions. He too walked away from a life of lies and was doing his best to start over—God's way. Shane was as big a messy miracle as I was.

His hand feels so good in mine, like a hot mitten just warmed. His eyes dance when he laughs. He's silly, so much fun, and makes me giggle. When he talks about the ranch he grew up on in Texas, his eyes glimmer and his whole face lights up.

His southern charm is enticing me. He serenades me in the car, plays DJ, picks me up every Sunday morning and takes me to church. He sits in his pickup with me for hours listening to me talk, like I'm the only one in the world who matters. He's got a big, generous heart and big, beautiful dreams. He's not the least bit overwhelmed by my pain; he's much stronger than I am. He's falling in love with me, and it feels like healing oil dripping down into the crevices of my heart.

I know early on, one day on the sandy beach in Mexico, who I'm dealing with. In a flash I see the golden hue of sun on the side of his face, and I know.

We have spent the better part of the day waiting our turn in the hot summer sand, watching two horses trudge up and down the beach carrying unsatisfied tourists on their backs. The horses' spirits are tired, and their speckled and spotted coats are heaving and sweating. As Shane and I sit on the beach watching this pathetic display, we lean in and whisper to each other, "I wonder if we could get those horses to run again."

When it is our turn we mount and kick them into action. And like lightning they bolt.

When the crowd on the beach sees those mangy horses coming at them in full gallop, they run for cover. With a smile and a nod, Shane points to the islands and we take off for the horizon. The insides of our thighs grip the horses' sides. Water sprays from descending hooves in crystallized beads and the wind lifts us under its wings. Riding on a speckled white stallion, Shane's thinking, I'm a cowboy—I know how to ride a horse, and there is no way this California girl is going to keep up with me. But when he turns his head to see how far he's left me in the dust, I am right there beside him, riding high and free.

The sun flashes its golden light on his cheek. I see the reflection on his face and my heart skips a beat, and I know I've found my prince.

I email my best girlfriend when I get back. "I met a guy named Shane. We rode horses on the beach, and I'm going to marry him!"

"Simmer down, upstart," she writes back, *"We're not living on* The Young and the Restless. *"*

"Oh, yes we are!" I respond. I have no intention of simmering down. The feeling gets stronger and stronger. Our souls' connection is undeniable, and finally the day comes for us—the day every girl dreams about.

Standing at the end of the aisle, I am dressed in white. The delicate, sheer fabric of my veil softly blurs my vision, but I can see all the way down the sunlit runway to my groom. Discovering just weeks before the wedding that my gown hung far too short, seamstresses added inches to the satin hem, extending the train with vines of hand-stitched embroidery, sequins, and pearls. My father carefully lifts back the veil, kisses my cheek, and I see in Shane's eyes the glisten of true love.

We carefully recite our vows, and then it's time to take the Body and the Blood. I fight back a flood of tears, trying not to smear all my wedding makeup. When I taste the cracker in my mouth, I remember how

God reached into the darkest place of my soul and offered me a whole new life. He performed an even greater work redeeming Shane. We tip the cups back and wine coats our throats. I am so grateful to be saved and loved and cherished like this, to be wearing white, and to have my groom wait for me and treat me like I was worth waiting for. This day is a miracle.

A Man or a Mirror?

It had been a long, broken road that led us both to that altar. Shane certainly did see a potential bride in me, and he definitely wanted to scoop me up in his arms and sweep me away to the castle. In fact, he redesigned our entire backyard of our new home before that wedding day so it would be a lush garden when I walked into it for the first time as his bride. He prepared that place for me.

And even though I came cleansed by faith into the marriage, there were still a lot of broken pieces buried at the floor of my heart. I still had the habit of making man my mirror, and as happens with many brides, I turned Shane into the prince who was supposed to be my perfect king for everything.

If he was having a great day and came home praising me—complimenting me on dinner, noticing how nice the house looked or I looked—I felt great. But if he didn't, I felt terrible—I thought he didn't see me or love me or something was wrong. Poor guy! If he was happy, I was happy. If he was grumpy, I was grumpy. If he was angry, I was angry. If he was playful, so was I. What a rollercoaster.

What I didn't realize was that even though Shane was my husband now, that didn't mean he was responsible for my happiness. Sometimes his mind just wasn't on me. He was thinking about other things. We had two babies in the first three years, so I was dealing with diapers and tantrums and he was dealing with work. We loved each other, but there were lots of days when we didn't exactly lavish each other with love the way we did when we were dating.

It is so easy to get confused with the *prince* thing. Like the princesses in the fairy tales, we think our husbands are the ones who are always going to tell us we are loved and valued and deserving of a hope and a future. We expect them to be responsible for our peace and joy, but we end up like a ship with no anchor, blown and tossed about.

When a woman makes a man her mirror, we do both him and ourselves an injustice. No man was ever designed to be the exact reflection of our value, beauty, worth, and purpose. Man and woman were never designed to define one another. So when we look to our husband to be the perfect reflection of our value, we are trying to get something from him he was never designed to give.

But when we both look to the Father for our reflection, we have more love to give. When we turn away from the mirror of what we can see to the mirror of what we can't see, our vision becomes 20/20. Everything crystallizes and through the glasses of the Word, we see exactly who man is, who God is, who we are, and what we need to know.

We must remember: God came as a man, and only his love can raise a dead girl to life.

2 The First Truth:

You Are a Beloved Daughter

*Hold on to what you have, so that
no one will take your crown.*

REVELATION 3:11

Man

I am weeping. These are not superficial tears. This is pain that runs
through the very fibers of my being.

There's so much misunderstanding and it's all a disharmony of confusing voices. Distrust, betrayal, truths, and lies—I cannot distinguish who
is right and who is wrong and what on earth I'm going to do about it.
I've tried to counsel, control, defend, and argue. I've yelled, I've screamed,
I've begged, I've reasoned. I've tried to repair this shattered picture that
has fallen off the wall and crashed to the floor. But I've only ended up
more hurt. My efforts have failed me and led to nothing but brokenness.

I land on my knees. On my knees, man is man and God is God. On
my knees, we are all fallen. The more I look at my circumstance the more
I grieve. But the more I look up, the more I see. He is on his throne, yet
so approachable that I crawl like a little girl into his lap. He wraps me
in his arms. I lean back between his shoulders and rest my head upon
his heart. All the striving in my body drains out of me and I weep and
rest and cry a little more…and I begin to relax.

I'm so very tired of wrestling with man. I just want to linger here on your lap, God. I want to sink in and feel your enormity, the way you know me and love me without fault. I want to drink in your sweet grace and taste your mercy and be baptized in the waters of your blood.

Holding me, he dips me back and immerses me. Grace in all its forms floods over me in waves. As I sink deeper yet, my soul is quieted. Through the beams of light I see his eyes, his mouth, his beard, and he's as big as the sky. And I feel him say to me, "I love you."

He supports my whole body, and as I rise back up from the waters, my chains fall to the ocean's floor in a heavy clank. Lighter, I come up and suck the air. Sweet beads of grace drip down my face. I feel washed all over, like I've been scrubbed from the inside out. I feel those unraveled and frayed fibers coming back together and fusing in a new pattern; he is tenderly reconstructing me.

My wounds remain raw but a cleansing tide is washing over them, rushing as a river over broken and imperfect stones.

Strength begins to flow through my veins.

When I stand up I feel like I can live again.

Man can sometimes seem so powerful, so important. He can whisper adoring words in our ear and the whole world goes silent. He can lash us with careless curses and scar the inner chambers of our hearts. He can lift up our entire body and soul just by looking in our eyes; yet his desertion or death can knock us to the floor. He can make our hearts skip with joy or weep with angst. We can allow his love to be our center, and the desire for his love, a breaking madness. We can allow him to protect us as a faithful shield or pierce us like a flaming arrow. When we fall, we long for him to stand, to hold out his hand and lift us from the ashes.

The impact man—and people in general—can have on us is weighty. When we look to man to tell us our value, we can end up full of mucky pride or empty as a discarded can. We can end up radically healed or sorely bleeding.

Man is made in the likeness of God, but he is not a god. Women are made in the image of God; we are not reflections of man. We are both the glory and crown of a man, his complement and completion; but he doesn't tell us who we are or weigh our worth like jewels on a scale.

Man is a mist, here one day and gone the next. In fact, God can blow his breath over a man and the man can fall down dead. "All men are like grass," Isaiah writes. "The grass withers and the flowers fall, because the breath of the LORD blows on them" (Isaiah 40:6-7). Like a flower, man rises, has his time of glory, and then fades and dies, sometimes slowly, sometimes in a gust of wind. In Psalm 144:3-4, David asks, "LORD, what are human beings that you care for them, mere mortals that you think of them? They are like a breath; their days are like a fleeting shadow."

From dust we came and to dust we return, and our spirits go back to God who made us. So man is impermanent—a breath, a shadow, a flower, grass. Yet, we need him. And he needs us.

I Am Woman

I want to see him look me in the eyes and light all up from within. I want him to love me. I want so badly to see it in his face. But he's worried now, about work. He can laugh and play but in the back of his mind, he's thinking about sustaining us.

He wants to buy me those new chairs, those shoes; he says the house needs a new roof and gutters to stand the coming rains; he longs to plant more trees and take me on that vacation I've been hoping for. He is a man, born to provide. But right now he can barely look me in the eye because he hates that it's been so hard.

But I am woman. All I want is his loving arms around me, my children safe at home. I do want those new chairs, I admit, and new shoes, and new clothes, and a vacation. But above all I long for his body next to mine, his hands weaving through my hair, his mouth pressing against my skin. I want to be lost in him and drown in his love. Eye to eye, heart to heart, soul to soul, I want to receive him like that, our love like a prayer. And we both want to laugh for a spell before the world begins its day.

We savor these moments, but most of the time it's not like that at all. It's just real life: the alarm clock wakes me to a baby crying, there's breakfast to make, school forms to sign, lunches to pack, children to dress and comfort, and a big yellow bus to wave goodbye to while our kids go off to another day of learning. I turn around and there are dishes to do, floors to clean, laundry to fold, a baby to care for, and a tired face in the mirror that takes too much work to make up pretty. For him, there are emails and texts, phone calls and meetings, trash to take out and gas tanks to fill, deals to get out of the starting gate and ride hard to the finish line. It's a whole new day of fighting for his place in this hard, hard world.

Sometimes we just don't have enough truth in our heads, and those lies from our pasts—the ones we were supposed to shed like chains in that baptismal water—start tripping us up. We wonder if we're going to make it. Yet we are married, so it's up to us to clean up the carnage of our hearts.

We land on our knees and our cries reach heaven's ears. The light streams into our darkened room. Love rises, mercy falls, and we are one again. Eye to eye, heart to heart, marriage like incense, the smoke of our prayers.

Before the fall, Eve's worth was embedded in God alone. Both she and Adam looked to him as a measure of their value. God provided all they needed; he was more than enough. But after their deceptive exchange with that lying serpent, everything went awry.

As a consequence, he cursed the serpent with his words. "You will crawl on your belly and you will eat dust all the days of your life," he declared, proclaiming there would be ongoing hostility between the serpent and the woman, and between his offspring and her offspring. "He will crush your head, and you will strike his heel" (Genesis 3:14-15).

Sometimes we experience hostility. It's painful just to get up in the morning, and throughout the day we feel like that wound is draining the strength from us with every step. Sometimes it feels like someone has gotten in our way, tripped us up in the middle of the pathways of marriage, motherhood, friendships, and relationships. Sometimes we fall flat on our face.

I wonder what it was like for Eve. I know that during her days on earth, Eve longed for a return to paradise, where she could walk with God and talk with him in the cool of the day; where she could love and be loved by her husband, unencumbered by selfishness and shame, deceit and despair.

Because the first humans chose to listen to their opponent over the voice of God, everything was altered. Fit or not in the mind of man, God's punishment was sure: Eve and every woman after her would experience sorrow and pain bearing their children. On top of it, women would possess an inordinate desire for their husbands.

Like Eve's, Adam's consequence fit his nature: he and every man after him would work by the sweat of their brows all the days of their lives. Through painful toil they would wrestle with the cursed earth. The soil would produce thorns and thistles which they would have to battle in order to sustain the treasure that was once so readily available. And after all of this, they were fated to return to the dust in death.

Therein lies our curse. As a result, men are naturally driven to look to their work for their value while women look to their husbands...when all along we were designed to look to God.

Eve Speaks

It was more confusing than you would think. I went off on my own. I wandered far from God and away from my husband. I should have never done that; they always provided the protection I needed. I began listening to the serpent and entertaining his slippery lies. I somehow concluded it was reasonable to ignore God's commands. I doubted his goodness, even though I knew full well his Word was perfect.

The snake promised me that I could have what I foolishly desired: more. More wealth, more wisdom, more knowledge, more power, more prowess. It was so tempting to believe that I could actually be like God in knowing what he knew.

The snake made it look so attractive, so beautiful even, to have that kind of power, to forge my own way.

But this was my foolishness: I had power available to me already! We were given dominion over the earth, the creatures of the sea, and the beasts of the field. I had authority! But that snake tapped into that place of longing in my soul that only God could fill. He made it seem like I would be "more" if I obeyed him. But I was already More! I had the Lord God available to me; I had access to more fulfillment than any woman could dream of having.

I am forgiven: I just want to say that up front. The lineage of my third son Seth led to the Redeemer, and through his blood we are all forgiven.

But it was paradise. We were encompassed by the most verdant garden you could imagine. I held the Lord God's hand! I heard the Lord God's voice. I walked with him on glistening stones!

How that wicked Lucifer could make that one piece of fruit look better than communion with my Father and perfect unity with my husband, I don't even know.

Our enemy is such a liar!

He tricked me.

I ate.

And then I offered the fruit to my husband and he ate too.

The dishonor, the disgrace, the shame. But I could not go back! God cursed that ugly snake on account of me and sent us out of paradise. How it tore our hearts!

Outside those gates, life was bitter. I know the heartbreak the Father felt mirrored our own. We were his first children. But all that time we spent outside that blissful garden, I held on to this:

> *I know that my Redeemer lives,*
>
> *And He shall stand at last on the earth;*
>
> *And after my skin is destroyed, this I know,*
>
> *That in my flesh I shall see God (Job 19:25-26).*

Men are only men, as fallible as you are. Men long just as deeply as you do to return to the garden, to rest complete and whole. They yearn to hear God's voice just as much as you do.

Pursue love, my sister. Pursue God. And then love the men in your life the way you are loved by the Father. As you receive, give.

Just remember, men are born sons of God, but they are not God—not at all! Man cannot fill your heart with the love that is necessary to survive. Only God can.

The Father

To discover who God is, we have to turn away from the mirror of man and fix our gaze on the one unchanging mirror.

Malachi 3:6 says, "I the Lord do not change." Numbers 23:19 says, "God is not human, that he should lie, not a human being, that he should change his mind. Does he speak and then not act? Does he promise and not fulfill?" Man's opinion can change. Even the best man can shift like a fleeting shadow. Man can make mistakes. Man can fall. Man can promise and not fulfill. Man can accuse or disappoint. He can leave us; he can choose another. And even the greatest, most faithful men die.

God, on the other hand, is our Rock, our loving ally, our strong-hold, our deliverer, our fortress, our high tower, our shelter and shade from the heat of the day, our refuge and hiding place from the storm and the rain (Psalm 144:1-2; Isaiah 4:6). Men were never designed to be this for us. It's simply too much for a man to be the rock, the refuge, and the hiding place. At times our husbands can feel like this to us, but that role cannot be sustained.

They may be wonderful reflections of the Father's love, but they are not the source of it.

Psalm 118:8-9 says, "It is better to take refuge in the LORD than to trust in humans. It is better to take refuge in the LORD than to trust in princes." A prince is a good man—a man who loves you, is faithful to you, believes in you, endures the storms of life with you, and fights with all his heart to protect you, care for you, provide for you, and assure you that you are loved.

But our prince can never be God.

The world is a stormy place, and the winds of change can trans-form our lives with one peal of thunder. In the blink of an eye, your lover can die. Your best friend can vanish. After a lifetime of devotion, your husband can leave you. I could go on—we all know about adul-tery and addiction and disease and death. We know man can betray us and even the best of men fall. So we'd better know the difference between a man who turns to dust and the Rock of our Refuge.

That Rock is God—but he is not only that. He is our Father (Isa-iah 64:8).

That one word—Father—is solid ground to some and a rattling earthquake for others.

The Father Speaks

Humans are made in my likeness, but they try to make me like them. This confuses you. If you make me in the image of restless man, I will never be enough to satisfy your yearning heart. Yes, some men reflect my image well; they teach you who I am through mirroring forgiveness, grace, patience, and a love that protects, believes, hopes, endures, and is couched in kindness and self-control. Yes, a man can be a picture of my love, but only my Son was perfected in love.

My dear one, do not form me in the image of your father. I am the Father who made your father. Somewhere along the way he may have created a new definition of me; in the mirror of that definition, you may feel that I am inaccessible, unreachable, condemning, or angry. You may feel that you are unworthy or unable to live out the dreams of your heart. Whether or not your father accurately portrayed my heart toward you, it's all right. I can fill in the gaps. Remember, it's human nature for man to try to define me in his own way.

But I want you to redefine who I am by looking into the mirror of my Word. I am your Provider, your Healer, and your Banner. And my banner over you is love.

I am the God who birthed you. As a father, I watch over all your comings and goings. I have seen every failure, every hurt, every victory, every valley, and every mountain you've traversed, and I know all too well the storms that have torn your precious heart. These are things your earthly father could never fully know. Come to me, my wearied daughter. I am here, waiting for you. You don't have to do anything but believe for me to be pleased with you.

Before my Son ever performed a miracle, before he ever fed the thousands, before he taught a single parable, and before he laid down his life, I spoke a word over him that I speak over you now: "This is my Son, whom I love. With him I am well pleased."

This is the life I want for you, daughter: to walk as one who knows she is my beloved, with whom I am well pleased, before you've done a single thing right.

Look away from the mirror of man; so often, his love is woefully incomplete. Look at me! See your true reflection in the mirror of me.

In my dealings with women, I've found that the most common wound we experience is from our fathers. Personally, I have seen how God can stand in the gap. When my earthly father wasn't present, my heavenly Father was; when my earthly father didn't understand me, my heavenly Father did; and where my earthly father fell short, my heavenly Father filled the areas of vacancy to overflowing.

At the same time, I believe that God worked through my earthly father to usher me toward a heavenly path. Without my father's encouragement to pursue modeling, I would have never seen and experienced all that I did—the good, the bad, and the ugly. Without his signature on that very first modeling contract, and his faith in what I do now, I wouldn't have the ministry that I do today.

I traversed this precarious world by myself at a young age, and I came across far too many men who didn't care whose daughter I was. The pain led me to my heavenly Father. I needed his protection, guidance, and healing—all of which he offered me. Since then, the injuries from my broken road have been restored to us a hundredfold as my story has served as a healing balm to others' shattered hearts.

We look far and wide to fill a void that is impossible for man to fill. But our personal experiences do not define our heavenly Father. God defines himself. And in the reflection of his face, we see who we are and what we are worth.

Baby Girl

There is a scene in the Old Testament that is a profound picture of the Father's heart toward a nation he deeply loves. He uses this image to remind us of his deep love for us. Ezekiel 16:1-14 describes Jerusalem as a dejected, unloved, and abandoned baby girl. Tossed aside in a heap as though disposable, the little baby girl is left to fend for herself. Kicking about and struggling as an infant would, she is naked, bare, and bloody, fighting for life when God passes by.

Your parents were pagans, he says. "On the day you were born your cord was not cut, nor were you washed with water to make you clean, nor were you rubbed with salt or wrapped in cloths. No one looked on you with pity or had compassion enough to do any of these things for you. Rather, you were thrown out into the open field, for on the day you were born you were despised.

"Then I passed by."

The Father sees the little girl when no one else does. Her cries echo in the heavenly realm, and his heart reaches out for her in compassion. He receives her just as she is, bloody and broken, and speaks life into her. "I…saw you kicking about in your blood, and as you lay there in your blood I said to you, 'Live!'"

He says the same thing to us. Man's rejection, abandonment, or neglect may leave us feeling bloody and broken, but God sees our hurt and desires to raise us from it.

God's presence breathes life into the baby girl, and she grows. Later, he passes by again, spreading the corner of his garment over her and covering her naked body, just as he did for Adam and Eve. He gives the girl his solemn oath and enters into a covenant with her, calling her "Mine."

His covenant is his bond: "Never will I leave you; never will I forsake you" (Hebrews 13:5). Once she was his daughter. Now she becomes his bride.

He rescues the little girl.

He repairs her, renews her, and restores her.

He redeems, reclaims, and renames her: "Mine."

Then, he bathes her with water and washes the blood from her and puts perfume on her. He clothes her with an embroidered dress, fine linen, costly garments, and leather sandals. He adorns her with jewelry, putting bracelets on her arms, a necklace around her neck, a ring in her nose, earrings in her ears, and a beautiful crown on her head.

He adorns her, not because of the beauty she already possesses, but because of the power of his love to beautify her.

"So you were adorned with gold and silver; your clothes were of fine linen and costly fabric and embroidered cloth." This shows right here that God loves a great outfit! He continues to lavish her: "Your food was honey, olive oil and the finest flour. You became very beautiful and rose to be a queen."

He readies his bride and releases her to reign, returning her to her rightful place in his kingdom, to a position of influence as she now serves to be a guiding light. "And your fame spread among the nations on account of your beauty, because the splendor I had given you made your beauty perfect."

His love perfects us. He affirms us where we have been abandoned, beautifies us where we have been belittled, and confirms our destiny despite our desperate state. The Father's heart shines as he raises us from the dust of our destruction to hold our heads high, wearing a sparkling crown of beauty. We are his destined daughters and together, his bedazzled bride.

Man cannot give us the identity of God's Beloved, nor can he remove it from us: it is who we are, as irrevocable as the Word. It is God's oath, his promise, his bond to us, and we are dealing here with a God who does not change his mind:

> God is not human, that he should lie, not a human being, that he should change his mind. Does he speak and then not act? Does he promise and not fulfill? I have received a command to bless; he has blessed, and I cannot change it (Numbers 23:19-20).

When he calls us his daughters, it is forever.

Voices of the Daughters

God, I know I should call you Father but I can't.
My father was so condemning.
My father was absent.

My father beat me and bruised me.

My father wasn't there when I called for help.

My father has no idea who I am or where I am.

My father wanted somebody else more than he wanted me.

Are men really made in your image, God? The ones who abused me and threw me out like refuse?

Why is my husband nothing like my father? He hurts me more than my father ever did.

He left me.

He lied to me.

He gave his heart to another woman and blames me.

With only six weeks' notice, he died, and I keep thinking he's going to walk in the door at six o'clock for dinner.

Where do I turn? I'm kicking in the rubble, alone and bleeding, a crying baby girl.

Do you see me here, God?

Man has torn my heart, and I don't know where to look for answers.

A Letter from our Father

My Daughter,

How I long to gather you in my arms. I know all too well the ways that man has left you, disappointed you, lied to you, and abandoned you to struggle. For some of you, man has been a hammer, smashing the precious stones I laid so carefully in the floor of your heart.

The weight of his burden can wrap itself around you like a heavy chain; it can sink you toward the bottom if you let it. It would have been better for those who hurt you to have been drowned in the heart of the sea. I can handle those who hurt you; just give them to me.

But now I'm saying to you, daughter, live! Be mine. Let me lift you up and carry you to the surface. Let me have your heart, for only I can repair it. Let me cover you with the corner of my velvet robe; let me be your blanket. Let me spread my hand over you and shade you from this storm, this rain, this lightning that is splintering your sky and breaking the earth beneath your feet.

Daughter, I am your high tower. I have so much for you. Come to me, my storm-tossed daughter. Come to me. There is healing beneath my wings.

Many of us have been so lacking in fatherly love that we struggle to know the depths of the Father's heart. Some of us have been abandoned, rejected, belittled, abused, or left to fend for ourselves. Others can't put their finger on why they hurt. And still others were "Daddy's little girl," which is who we all wanted to be.

Mark 14:36 tells us that at the time of Jesus's most intense need, as he was heading toward the cross, he fell to the ground in the garden, crying, "*Abba*, Father!"

Abba means "Daddy." The pain was so intense that his blood vessels broke and he sweat drops of blood. At his gravest moment, he cried, "Daddy!"

When some of us see the words *Father* and *Daddy* side by side like that, we disconnect. The protective canopy of the father combined with the joyful companionship of the daddy? For many of us, these are a mismatch.

As children, we have unquestioning trust for the daddy. As adults, we have to get back in touch with who that is. Some of us sorely need a new picture of our heavenly *Abba* that heals our hearts and transforms the way we see ourselves.

I give you this picture of my husband and our daughter not because there's perfection in our home but because it's a profound picture of the daddy–daughter relationship.

He carries our brand-new baby girl up the narrow walkway to the front door. As I follow behind him, he has her wrapped tightly in her white blanket, patterned with speckled red lady bugs. He is holding her close to his heart like she is the most delicate creature he's ever laid his hands on, which, of course, she is. She is his daughter.

When he reaches the doorstep, he suddenly stops and grips her closer to his chest.

"What am I going to do when some guy comes knocking at the front door for her?" He panics. He is probably picturing himself with a rifle, standing between that future boy and his daughter's heart. He is dead serious about guarding her heart, and he knows full well that also means guarding her body. He is her father and that comes as naturally to him as hunting deer.

Of course, my concern at that point is not her dating.

"She is three days old," I say, ushering him through the doorway. "All she needs right now is a nap!" I shoo him along and put her down in her crib, in the beautiful room we have prepared for her.

We call Olivia our little lady bug. At night she curls up on Daddy's chest and sleeps with her head on his beating heart. He strokes her back and looks down at her and smiles so warm.

When Olivia is just 18 months old, Daddy starts taking her on dates. He calls her from work and asks her on a proper date, and she accepts. When the evening comes, he is dressed very nicely. He approaches her bedroom door right on time.

Olivia never wants him to see her until she is completely ready; she is like a princess in her chamber. I do her hair and she puts on her favorite outfit. Sometimes it's pink cowboy boots and jeans, sometimes a flowered sundress, sometimes black patent shoes, a woven sweater, and a satin skirt. No matter what, she prances out like she is the most prized child in the whole wide world.

On their dates, Daddy opens the door for her. Daddy notices her outfit and compliments her smile. Daddy takes her someplace special and they eat something yummy. Daddy asks her questions and looks her in the eye and listens for her answers. Whether it's pizza and pin-ball, the fair, a dance, or gourmet pasta with toasty bread dipped in sweet oil, for that moment, there is nothing in all the world that matters more than her.

They never skip dessert. It could be ice cream or warm gooey cookies or a chocolate soufflé that oozes out in a heavenly drizzle. No matter what, their time together is marked by friendship and laughter and holding hands and fun: it's a daddy–daughter date.

At the end of the evening, they buy flowers for her and Mommy too.

When Olivia is tucked in and I finish arranging her flowers so she can see them from her bed, I lean over to kiss her goodnight. I can see in her face the radiance of knowing she is loved. She is adored. She is cherished. She is Daddy's choice.

Of course in the back of his mind, Shane is thinking, "If some guy doesn't pick her up on time or tries to text her for a date or doesn't open the door for her or tries to get away with not paying for her meal or treating her like a princess, she'll know who to call! She'll call me, and I'll come rescue her from that fool!"

You don't have to have an earthly daddy to know your heavenly Daddy's heart for you. When we put our faith in his Son, the Father comes and makes his home in us by giving us his Spirit. By this Spirit, we can all cry, "*Abba,* Father!" because whether or not you were "Daddy's little girl" on earth, you are in heaven.

When our daughter Olivia was two years old, she began to suffer from fears. She said she saw an image of a bad man through her window one night and claimed that he reached out to grab her. We were never able to confirm it, but for the next two long years, she became wracked with fear. Every night before she went to bed, she asked if the man was going to come through her window to hurt her. Of course Daddy would check the locks and promise her she was safe, and I would assure her there was nothing to be afraid of. And every morning she would wake up unharmed. But the next night she would recite her same fear. No matter what we did, her fears were on the edge of her lips.

After two years of repeating the same nightly conversation, I changed her sleep ritual. As she lay in her bed, instead of entertaining her fears, I began to go on and on about how much she was loved. I covered her with kisses from head to toe while she giggled and laughed, and before she could even ask me about the "bad man," I whispered in her ear, "You are my special girl."

As I began to walk out of the room, my little four-year-old daughter opened her mouth again to say she was afraid, but I just repeated how much I loved her.

These statements of love broke her recourse of fear. And these are the very words God whispers in your ear the moment you put your heart in his hands, and every day thereafter: *You are my special girl.*

No matter how you feel right now, you are his special girl. You are his child: that is your security. You are his beloved: that is your confidence. You are his daughter: that is your beauty and your value.

In the writings of the apostle John, he never called himself "John." Instead, he called himself "the one the Lord loved." Did he think he was more special than Matthew, Mark, or Luke? Was he full of himself? No. He just knew how wide, how deep, how wonderful was the love of Christ. John so rooted himself in the Lord's love, he saw it as his identity.

From the tips of your toes to the crown on your head, you are the one the Lord loves. Deuteronomy 33:12 says, "Let the beloved of the LORD rest secure in him, for he shields him all day long, and the one the LORD loves rests between his shoulders."

There are times when we need to crawl into Daddy's lap and rest between his shoulders. There are times we need to cry and let him hold us and shield us. And there are times when we need to rise from the ashes and hold our heads high, knowing we wear the crown of the redeemed. But when we are always looking at the past, at how man has hurt us, we end up living as victims instead of victors. It's easy to be a victim, but it doesn't honor the king who rescued us from the rubble.

The Crown

"The daughter of the King is not a victim, Jen," Deborah says to me, her turquoise eyes clear as crystal.

Funny that she would say that, because I have a beautiful jeweled crown I often put on my head to show others the daughter's value.

"You are angry," she challenges me.

Her words are like a lightning bolt that knocks the broken stones of my heart loose. I start to cry. I am angry. I feel forsaken by men, abandoned, discarded, used, and dismissed.

Sometimes God puts angels in our paths to set forth a storm in our hearts. This one sends me running for the lighthouse, desperate for cover.

God is our Father, but he is also our fortress, our high tower, our deliverer.

As the sky peals with lightning and thunder, I run to the lighthouse like a little girl, my broken umbrella bent backward by the force of the wind.

Faith in Christ is the key to the lighthouse door, and I use it and dump the treasure chest of my heart in a heap on the entry floor. My broken stones scatter everywhere. I have to look at them. I have to see what has made my heart so hard in places, so bitter in others. I have to see what has stolen my joy and who has robbed my peace and why I am still living like a victim.

Jesus is standing there, ready to sift through my broken stones. Kindly, he places them all back in the treasure chest and takes the first step toward the top of the lighthouse. I follow. On that step, he holds out one jagged stone, soiled by grime. I turn away at the painful memory. He tells me that he was there, that he saw how I was kicking about in the rubble. I can't clean the stone myself; only he can polish it. In a tidal wave, I forgive my offender because I know he is the judge.

We take more and more steps, sorting through the stones one by one. It seems like we spend whole seasons just on one handful of broken stones. But the more we consider the film of anger that is covering the jewels of my heart, the more I let his living water wash them, and I cry, "I forgive him, Father…I forgive him." And I hand my broken pieces to my deliverer.

At one point I grab the chest from his hands and try to carry its weight myself, thinking I can do it, I can sort it out on my own, but instead of getting farther I fall and all the stones spill again, and I cry. I can't do it without you, Jesus. I can't sort through this mess, I say. At times like this, he invites others to come and help me pick up the pieces.

Higher up the staircase, I stare for too long at one set of crushed stones. Anger, accusations, and blame spurt from my mouth. He takes them all in bodily; he understands betrayal and rejection.

The biggest step is still ahead, but I have to climb it if I want to see the view from the top. I have to stop blaming everyone else and look at how I broke and soiled my own heart and how I hurt others. Other people's stones are not mine to carry. So I trade forgiveness for forgiveness, mucky jewels for clean ones, and take the final step to the top.

When I get to the landing of the lighthouse, I can see the view of the hot red sun resting on the indigo sea. Jesus is behind me now, doing something with my jewels. I am looking out at the horizon. I see past the storm. I smile at the future.

He places the crown of jewels on my head and says, "Keep your chin up so it won't fall off."

As daughters of the King, we have to wear our crowns well. Princes don't give us crowns; they are an inheritance from the King. As no man can give them to us, no man can take them away. But they may get jaded, or crooked, or lost if we aren't careful.

A woman just wouldn't let a man abuse her with a crown on her head. She wouldn't cut herself. She wouldn't get high and wasted; she wouldn't give her body away as if it were free. She wouldn't curse the people in her own family and she wouldn't carry the weight of their stones on her back. The Daughter of the King is a victor, not a victim. She is destined for glory.

Not only do we need to wear our crowns well, but we need to, by example, teach our daughters to do the same. We are not princesses to be served, but princesses who come to serve.

The King of Kings Speaks

I wore a crown of piercing thorns so you could wear a crown of priceless jewels, my daughter.

I wasn't the kind of king they were looking for, you know. I was much smaller. They thought I would come like a supernova shooting through the night sky. They thought I would come as a commanding ruler in authority and majesty.

But I came like a dimly lit candle, a small, flickering light—just as you came, a newborn baby. There was no room for me in the inn.

In my time as a man, I found there was little room in the world for me either. There I was, the Son of Man, in skin. Though some of my brothers recognized me right away and loved me, many more mocked and insulted me. Most despised me. Their hearts were hard.

Perceiving this, I revealed myself to them in miracles, healings, and displays of power. But so few received me. So few knew my heart.

I was Emmanuel, God Come Down. I came like they did, in humility, so they would know that I understood their sorrow and their shame, their burdens and their flesh.

They pictured me as enthroned with a king's scepter. But they got a carpenter. *They got a common man who could read their hearts and minds and who called God "Father." This threatened them.*

They expected a ruler, but got a servant; a holy lord, but got a hilltop preacher; a saint, but got a friend of sinners; a king, but got a champion of the lowly. They expected more, but I made myself less.

They saw me on a throne, the train of my robe filling the temple with glory; they got a man, beaten, bloody, smitten by God, and hated by priests. When I refused their trickery they whipped me senseless and crowned me an unglorified king of the Jews, the piercing crown of thorns breaking my Father's heart.

With each lashing, I felt your rejection, your suffering. I felt the way you were abandoned and alone, even the way you felt separate from God. I felt what it's like to long for man's love and not get it. I know what it feels like to love so deeply, so hard, so raw, and so real and yet be spit upon. I know what it feels like to offer forgiveness but in turn be condemned.

To give grace as man turns his face.

To bless and be cursed.

To long to unite men to the Father and not succeed.

And I know what love is: believing, trusting, suffering long, and never giving up.

And I also know the inheritance that awaits you, Daughter.

Live to please me. Get behind the men in your life by laying your crown at their feet like I did. I didn't use my authority like a sword. I used it to serve others in love. Likewise, you too can lay down your life for your friends.

I will come back for you like a supernova blazing through the blue-black sky. You'll know me when you see me. On my thigh and on my robe I have this name written: KING OF KINGS AND LORD OF LORDS.

"I am coming soon. Hold on to what you have, so that no one will take your crown."

3 The Second Lie:

You Are What You See in the Mirror

*I used to think the mirror was a perfect reflection, but
now I know it couldn't be. It's always changing.*

Magic Mirror on the Wall

I fell to the temptation to get eyelash extensions. They just looked too pretty in the picture on the wall. That day I went all-out for me and got an over-the-top foot massage, mani/pedi, and lip, eyebrow, and chin wax. I felt like a million bucks when I shuffled out of the salon, tissue between my toes, eyelashes like butterflies brushing sticky eyelids.

When I got home I made the foolish mistake of examining my reflection in the wrong mirror—the one that hangs in the hallway outside the baby's room. It has this wicked way of highlighting every flaw. If I had my druthers I'd have everlasting Botox or whatever concoction they've invented to make the lines disappear. I'd have an anti-aging peel that takes ten years off my face without looking like it's been blistered and beat. I'd have teeth whitened in an instant, dark roots touched up and hair semi-glossed, laser hair removal. I'd like to be smooth forever.

In a perfect world I would also have custom workouts with a personal trainer, become magically tan without looking like a sweet potato pie, take two-hour yoga classes, and have regular hot stone massages. I would also have a flat stomach, fantastic breasts, and a rear end that stands up like it has something to say—all without pain, surgery, doctor bills or follow-ups. I'd like it all, please, without cost. And of course I don't want anyone to know I've done a thing to myself, especially my own daughter. Can we make it look "natural"?

Somehow I doubt it. "Mom, did you get eyelashes?" she asked the moment she saw me. How did I think I was going to get this past her or anybody?

"You look like a cat! Stop doing all these ridiculous things to yourself!" my mother-in-love said. Good thing I like her.

I secretly tried to trim the lashes to look real without chopping off my own, but the fake lashes criss-crossed and clumped and stabbed me in the eye. Half of them fell out and the other half wouldn't budge. My husband tried to pipe in, "I like 'em," but I was too worried about what the women at my next conference were going to think! Were they really going to listen to a thing I had to say about beauty while I had three sticky eyelashes clinging like a spider to my eye?

The mirror is always changing.

After three kids I'm left with a C-section scar that looks like a stitch across a pillow, eyes that can barely see without contacts, hair half as thick as it used to be, a host of wonder-bras, and a heart full of memories. To be honest I haven't lifted weights much this year, but I've lifted my baby a thousand times, I've lifted my family when it seemed like we might all fall, and I've loved well. Not perfectly, but well.

It's too bad I looked in that wretched mirror that day. When I do that, I can get all confused and think it's a reflection of me.

But a mirror on a wall could never tell us who's the fairest of them all.

Happy Now?

I needed to get into the mindset of an anorexic girl, even though I was one. I Googled "diary of an anorexic," and their blogs popped up. Like Alice descending a tubular slide, I tunneled into the worlds of girls with eating disorders. Page after page, site after site, blog after blog: their begging words were riddled with photographs of bone-thin bodies. These aren't starving African children. No, in a world where women would kill to feed their babies, these girls are intentionally starving themselves. I am bombarded by images of hollow tummies framed by ribs and sexy bikini bottoms, undernourished arms, and too-thin thighs. One girl even has the impossible body with a picture of Barbie pasted over the face. The caption reads, "Happy Now?"

The images are their goals. The bodies are their aspirations. Their "likes" tell me so much about them. The anorexics egg each other on—comparing, competing, compelling one another to starve. Full websites enable them to trade tips on how to be anorexic and calculate their "ideal" measurements, body mass index, and weight.

What they don't know is there is not a scale on earth which gauges the weight of who they are.

Their screen names are "skinnylove," "barbiebody," "bonesandboobs."

"You are borderline anorexic!" one girl writes in her online diary, quoting her tormented mother who is screaming from the bottom of the stairs, begging her to come down for dinner. But the girl rebels at the threat of evil food, as she did the night before and the night before. The girl's mother is at a loss for what to do.

"Borderline anorexic?!!" the girl writes, "What black hole has she been living in?!! I'm NOT going down there. All I want to do is sleep…"

I remember this. I remember going to sleep hungry. I remember the darkness, the rebellion, the distance I put between myself and goodness. I remember starving myself to please a man, and how I could not see who I was, what I was made of, and the wretch I was becoming.

Nina wraps the measuring tape around my waist, cinching it closed with the clink of her porcelain nails: 28"

She pencils the numbers on her notepad.

Breasts: 36"

Waist: 28"

Hips: 36"

Sliding the silver weight of the scale, click, click, tap: 141.

Height: 6'

"I'd like to see you lose two inches in your waist, one and a half inches in your hips, and get down to 125," she says matter-of-factly. "That would be ideal."

"How is she going to lose fifteen pounds? Where can she take two inches off her hips?" my father asks, as if someone is going to pipe up and agree with him.

"Working out," she announces in her I-know-this-business-don't-question-me tone. "Swimming is the absolute best way to shed pounds."

Neither Mom, nor Dad, nor I challenge the empress of the modeling world. Obviously, I will need to obey her.

"Now, mark my words,"—she shakes her finger at us—"she'll be on the cover of Vogue *by the end of the summer."*

All six of our eyes get big.

I'd better start running, I think, or find myself a pool.

Five summers later I am standing on the scale in the gym in Milan, having now signed with eight agencies around the world. Carefully, I

tap the silver bar to the left, to the left, to the left, transcending Nina's number by a longshot.

"There you go, Nina," I whisper. "Happy now?"

I look over my shoulder to make sure no one sees me and sneak into the steam room. Naked, I sit, spine hunched forward, long fingers gripping what's left of my thighs. I run my hands over the hollow curve of my empty belly and along the undergirding of my rib cage. I can feel each bone but still pinch the stubborn flesh clinging around my bellybutton.

It started out just losing college weight. Running, fat burners, yoga, carrot juice, cutting carbs, compulsive cardio. When I departed for Italy, I was fit, tan, and strong. Now I'm emaciated, pale, and weak.

People keep telling me I should eat, that I've lost weight in my face, that I look skeletal, that a man couldn't possibly love me like this. But I don't care. I don't want to eat. I'm not hungry. I'm not.

But I am. I am famished for none of this to matter, for the flesh around my middle to be all right. That's where I carry my organs, after all, and shouldn't women be allowed to have that? I'm so hungry for someone to look into my eyes and tell me I'm beautiful—not because of what they can see, but because of who I am. I'm so hungry to laugh and eat and frolic and play and for no one to care how the clothes hang on me.

I'm so used to being hungry. I'm starving to live in a world where the size of my breasts isn't a measurement of my likability. I'm starving to live in a world where big thighs are gorgeous and it doesn't matter if I'm curvy or straight. I want to be loved for more than how I look…but I believe that how I look is the only way to get love.

Beauty is expendable. As elusive as grains of sand, beauty slides from our grasp. The more we try to hold on to it, the more it sifts through our fingers. It cannot be seized. Not in this bathroom mirror, not here, not where my reflection is riddled by flaw, always less than perfect.

Mother Teresa once said, "The hunger for love is much more difficult to remove than the hunger for bread."

Pay Attention to Me

It is Fashion Week, and I am running through the Giardini Pubblici, the central park of Milan. I am pushing myself to sprint around the foot trails, avoiding eye contact with the happy couples licking gelato, gnawing lazily on their pizza, relaxing on their picnic blankets while their dogs tumble on the grass. Children toddle about, giggling, their faces slopped with gelato. But I have no time or energy to waste longing for what they have. I have to run. I have to be strong. It's showtime, and thousands of models are in town. They will all be vying for their place on the stage. I must claim what is mine.

Fashion Week is a sight to see. Packs of females stride the sidewalks of the fashion district, their toned legs and high heels more fascinating to watch than any finely-dressed mannequin in a Gucci store window. The models' lank bodies are draped all over the sidewalk cafes. They are either fresh-faced, inexperienced, and innocent as sweet whipped cream, or self-assured, chiseled, and qualified veterans who aren't begging for anybody's love. They've earned their place on the catwalk and they'll bump you off if you try to steal their place.

By day the models crowd the agencies, casting rooms, and foyers, gripping their portfolios, touching up their makeup, and reviewing their appointment books. By night they banter over glamorous dinner parties, consorting with Italian men at tables adorned with half-eaten plates of risotto, bruschetta, and frutti di mare. Many keep the party going, dancing suggestively until three in the morning in pulsing neon-lit clubs. It's a seductive parade...and underneath it's all a masquerade.

My journey through Fashion Week is uneventful until I meet the king of this play: Giorgio Armani. His sky blue eyes, silvery hair, sunbaked skin, and judicious gaze are validated by his exquisite suit, the cuffs perfectly coiffed and framing his manicured hands.

By a twist of fate I am no longer circling the streets of Milan looking for work; I am exploring Armani's empire.

He pays attention to me. He likes my skeleton frame. He chooses to design the makeup and hair for the shows on the palette of my head; he uses me to announce his new line to the press; he picks me to be first to step on the stage.

When I look in the mirror at Armani's studios, I am more because he wants me.

But after the shows I keep up the lifestyle of eccentric starvation and obsessive exercise; now I know no other way. All but Armani begin to tell me I've dropped weight, I appear tired; I should vacation. But they are wrong. I am booked solid for months.

Yet other designers complain that the fabrics drape off me as from a wire hanger; it threatens to be problematic that I don't fill out the tops, the pants, the gowns. Makeup artists snicker at my bones, muttering under their breath that I am sick. I am critiqued, analyzed, rejected, and discarded by more and more men whose job is to choose the right girl for the right clothes for the right picture. Some of them are seemingly unaware that my heart might be connected to my body. Others are simply looking for the right mannequin, and it's not their fault that it makes me feel small when I am not enough of what they want.

I all but race home for Christmas to get my bearings. When I step off the plane, my father is shocked by my dark and hollow eyes and withered stature. The depression reeks from me like the scent of mildewed rags.

Expressing concern about the cystic acne emerging on my chin, cheeks, and forehead, my parents make me an appointment with my childhood pediatrician.

I stand before him barefoot on the cold tile of his office, the childish wallpaper an echo from a simple past. His brow cinches as he examines not only the glaring pimples on my face but the muddy color of the circles around my eyes. His old, calloused fingers run along the spine of my back and brush my upper arm and lower leg. As he examines me, I believe he is looking for that little girl who used to bound into his office with blonde pigtails and big, wide sapphire eyes.

"What can we do about these pimples?" my mother and I ask—they are becoming far too inconvenient for a model.

He scans the sores on my face. "For these, I can prescribe antibiotics—tetracycline. It will take time, but they will eventually clear." He wraps his fingers around my forearm. "It's not her skin I'm worried about. It's her weight." His brow furrows. "What is also trouble- some is the foul odor of her breath. Are you ingesting chromium?"

"Yes," I answer. My fat burners are mostly made up of chromium picolinate.

"You are taking far too much. When was the last time you menstruated?"

"I can't remember," I respond. "Maybe six months ago."

His aged face and concerned eyes divert to my mother. "Does she have to go back to Europe?" he asks, troubled.

Of course we believed I did. None of us wanted to face the fact that I was beginning to suffer from anorexia. We all believed the Armani spring shows were too important and that I had to go back—I had a commitment. A veil covered our eyes. Either we could not see or did not want to see what that doctor saw so clearly.

Why does the world tug so hard on us that we refuse to address the most important thing, the truth standing in front of us?

It is eighteen years later and I am writing this book. I am study- ing anorexia and reading the blogs. I am wanting more than any- thing to offer answers to the hurting.

At this time there has been a circumstance in my life that has spun so out of control, been so painful, and become so challenging that I have not been eating. I, who have this ministry; I, who teach on women's beauty and bodies and identity and value. My pain is manifesting itself physically, as it did back then.

I catch it right away. Not eating as a response to stress is a temp- tation for me; maybe it always will be. This is my weakness: I want the world around me to be perfect and it's not, and people are not, and somehow I think if I can just be perfect I can heal it. It starts this time by fasting for spiritual reasons; it ends when I step back and see myself teetering on a very dangerous tightrope.

Maybe if I just get skeletal everyone in my world will bend to my demands, I think. Maybe if I stop eating altogether, if I go on a hunger strike, God will once and for all give me what I'm asking for. Maybe someone will pay attention.

Shane is holding me in front of the mirror, analyzing the width of my body next to his. He is brushing his hands over my ribs in concern. He is telling me to see a doctor. He is holding me and he cares.

I feel myself teetering on a narrow bridge and if I just tip slightly to the left, I will spiral and spin. But I can't spin; I cannot fall; there is too much at stake. I have a daughter now! I have two sons to live for! And I can't get up there to speak on the stage, a skeleton, a liar.

So I refuse.

I am a fighter, and I have more truth in my head than lies. I don't have a victim spirit; I have a spirit of victory. Yet we all crawl through mud sometimes before we stand on a hilltop; we all cross deserts and feel parched midway.

When Shane stands up and fights for me, I am relieved; I am loved.

Yet at the ocean floor of my heart I still wish someone stood up and fought relentlessly for me when I was Barbie. And then I remember that God fought for me—God did. When I didn't know what to do; God did. When humans offered me more worldly praise, God offered me his Son. In the middle of my sickness, he doctored my soul.

In Mark 5:24-34, we see a story of a bleeding woman and a God who heals.

The Bleeding Woman Speaks

I am tossing and turning on my bed; bleeding, as always. The bleeding is from my body but it feels like it's from my heart. It's an endless cramp, a steady groan. It's uncomfortable, uncontrollable, uncontainable, and ugly.

I'm the one with the filthy body that won't cooperate. No one will love me like this. No one will touch me. From the furthest corner of the cave of my heart, I am curled up and crying.

What is my life worth if I am a stinking bloody mess? I've endured twelve long years of endless bleeding. Is this my destiny? Shamed, spoiled, stained? Wrestling in the prison of this body, I scream for a way out. I have tried everything, spent everything I have.

It's in the silence of this torment that I hear a word whispering to me: Reach for the Healer.

In a flurry, I get up from my bed and clean myself. Quickly, I fasten the rags and dress, making sure no stain will leak through the robe.

I hurry outside and see the last of the evening light disappear from the horizon. The dusty streets are a bustle of activity. People are walking this way and that, most of them going home but many heading toward the lake, where the Healer is rumored to be.

The closer I get to the lakeside the more the crowds press around me. Everyone is trying to get to him. It feels like they're going to close in and crush me, but I weave and duck and press in and believe. I'm going all the way to the Healer tonight and no one's going to stop me.

It's wall-to-wall people when I get near. This is when I could give up. This is when I could say it's too hard. There are too many who want his attention! He doesn't have room for me. But I refuse. I am a fighter, and I have more truth in my head than lies.

Faith conquers fear, and suddenly the path before me breaks wide open and I can see his white robe, the edges billowing out like the wings of a dove. It's like the parting of the sea, and there is nothing between him and me now. I reach out to touch him, believing he will heal me.

My fingers grasp the edge of his garment and I grab a hold. As quickly as I reach for him his power reaches back for me. Warm healing floods through my body in a massive tidal wave. In the moment of our exchange, my torment flees. What miracle is this?

I shrink back into the crowd. Who cares if others reject me now? He has received me. He knows me! My heart races. I could throw myself face-down on the ground or faint or race through this crowd or leap or fall weeping. I feel so many things at once.

His followers try to usher him on, telling him to get away from all these bothersome people, but he is looking for me. He wants to see my face.

"Who touched me?" he asks, scanning the crowd. How does he know, when I only gripped the edge of the fabric?

I can hardly believe he wants to see me. I'm terrified that if he sees my face he will see my pain, and no one ever wants to look at my pain.

But I know this is God because it's running through my veins. Healing is a wild river and I've got my feet standing in it now. I cast all fear behind my back and fall shaking at his feet. I tell him everything: the whole truth. I leave nothing out—not one detail.

His gaze fixes on me—little me, messed-up me, soiled me whom nobody wants. He looks me in the eyes, his face awash with love and compassion—the most beautiful reflection I have ever seen. He looks through my imperfect body, his eyes touching my shredded heart.

"Daughter," he says, "your faith has healed you. Go in peace and be freed from your suffering."

I am healed; I am whole. I know it's just the beginning, that he will stitch together the torn fabric of my heart. I know he will keep on healing me.

I can still see my reflection in his eyes: Daughter. Healed.

The daughter is in communion with the Father and the Son. The Father loves her; the Son understands her.

The Son knows what it is to have pain in the body. The Son understands the perfection expected of women and girls. In the body, he knows abuse. He knows pain. He knows suffering.

Reaching out for the Healer is the beginning; continuing to reach is the journey of your life. You have gifts and talents and abilities that will only grow greater if you care for the flesh that holds them.

When I am tempted to go back to my old ways, abusing my body as a way to grasp control, I stop. I pursue no matter how hard it gets. I reach, believing. I hand him what I cannot control. I tell the whole truth. And he looks back at me, and says, kindly: "Daughter, your faith has made you well. Go in peace, and be healed of your affliction" (Mark 5:34 NKJV).

We are faced with a generation of girls afflicted by the lie that they *are* their bodies, they *are* what they see in the mirror. We cannot ignore the lies and hope they will go away. We must look those girls square in the eye and feed their soul hunger.

Never Enough

If eating disorders are indicative of a hole in the soul more so than a hole in the belly, how is that hole formed? In many cases, the natural need for approval becomes titanic when unmet.

My friend Gayle spun into an eating disorder when her older brother told her she would be beautiful if she grew her hair out and lost ten pounds. She did what he said, but in her search for approval, there was no destination point. *At what point am I good enough? At what point am I beautiful?*

At five feet eight inches and a healthy weight, Gayle dropped to a staggering 98 pounds. Always longing for her father's love, Gayle received nothing but rejection and disapproval from him. When he abandoned her family to start a new one, Gayle's mother grew morbidly obese, depressed, and disengaged. Rejecting her mother's mode of response, Gayle starved herself and then became bulimic to hide her illness, binging and purging on Big Macs and desserts sometimes fifteen times a day. When she did try to get her mom's attention, criticism cut her to the core.

"I was never good enough," Gayle winces. At 48, it still hurts.

We long for Daddy but Daddy does not want us; we long for Mom but Mom can't hear our cries. We long for approval, yet when conditions are placed upon that approval, we believe we are worth wherever we land on the measuring stick of the standards set for us.

When our lives spin out of control, we are like girls at amusement parks holding on for dear life. If we can control something—like what goes into our bodies—we feel like everything is going to be okay.

But we cannot control others, and even though we trick ourselves into thinking we can control our bodies, we cannot. Instead, the issues with food control us and start to suffocate us, becoming the full focus of our lives. As Gayle says, "The rope you're holding onto suddenly becomes a noose."

Loneliness is also one the greatest culprits in eating disorders. At the deepest points of my battle with anorexia, I felt completely alone and isolated—like I was on an island calling for someone to row their boat to me and take me away from the aloneness, but no one clearly heard my cries.

The biggest problem is I didn't cry loud enough, and I didn't cry to the right people. I muted my cries because I didn't want to admit I was sick. So I played the masquerade. I pretended the problem wasn't there.

Whether our desire to whip our bodies into submission comes from the need to control, the longing for approval, the desire for attention, or the blow of abandonment, it is further compounded by our image of beauty as sculpted by the culture. The culture defines for us what the reflection in the bathroom mirror should look like. The world of fashion shapes the image of perfection. As I worked in that world, I could easily model for catalogs and TV commercials at a healthy weight. But when it came to the runway, anorexia was my only viable option for entry. Today, the standards are even worse, and the models look less and less like natural women. Whether we want to admit it or not, it affects us.

When how we look takes precedence over our own happiness, we are not fulfilled. When it's all about how we compare to other women, we are worshipping idols. As we compare ourselves to others, we are never more for it. We are always less.

"*Not enough* is the main thing I hear," my friend April tells me as we ponder the issue of our unsatisfying bodies over a bag of delectable dark chocolate almonds. April has birthed four beautiful girls, is an aerobics instructor, and has recently lost 40 pounds. For the first time in years she weighs what she did in high school.

As I enjoy the company of this beautiful woman looking back at me, April talks about her body image. "I'm not thin enough, my breasts are not big enough, my stomach is not flat enough, my thighs are not small enough, and it eats at me from the first moment in the morning to the end of the day. I stand there in my aerobics class and compare myself to every other woman in the room. I stand there on the scale and get so ticked. But then I have to remind myself that there are children starving on the other side of the world. I have *seen* starving people. And I have to get a grip because I'm letting the fact that I've gained two pounds trash my day."

Over 80 percent of women are unsatisfied with their appearance, and 50 to 70 percent of healthy girls think they are overweight.[1] Only 2 percent of women believe they are beautiful.[2] One study found that "on average, women have 13 negative body thoughts daily—nearly one for every waking hour. And a disturbing number of women confess to having 35, 50 or even 100 hateful thoughts about their own shapes each day."[3]

If our goal is satisfaction with our bodies, we are in major trouble. The mirror, the jeans, and the scale are never satisfied, ever. Gayle, for instance, was long over her eating disorder when she got breast cancer. Having always been complimented on her long red hair and great figure, she had a double mastectomy and lost her hair.

Identifying her worth with her appearance during her cancer battle would have been toxic for her.

We are not in control of our bodies! We can exercise and eat right, but disease can strike any of us at any moment. I know a woman who, six months after she got married, contracted a strange virus that led to the amputation of all four of her limbs. This young bride is carried by her husband to the closet every morning and has to strap on arms and legs. You try to tell her that her body is her value! You try to tell her that her goal in life is to be satisfied with her body! That's a boldfaced lie from the pit of hell.

A whopping 97 percent of women report having at least one "I hate my body" moment each day, and over half of American women say they *despise* their bodies.[4] "Despise" is a powerful word. These women regard their bodies as worthless. They view them as trash.

Do you know what the body is a symbol for in the Bible?

The church.

Do you know who hates the church?

The devil.

Who do you think convinced me that starvation was a means to an end? Who do you think convinced Gayle that her need for love could be met by smaller-sized pants? Who do you think is whispering in April's ear during aerobics, telling her that she is not enough? Who do you think is lying to God's daughters, telling them that their value is reflected in the bathroom mirror?

Not God, I guarantee you. Not God.

Let's call a spade a spade. According to Ezekiel 28:12, Satan was the "seal of perfection, full of wisdom and perfect in beauty," whose heart became proud on account of his outward appearance. He didn't want people to focus on God. He wanted people to focus on him, on how beautiful, wise, and wealthy he was. Although he stands condemned by Christ's finished work on the cross, at this time he is the "prince of this world" (John 16:11). Naturally, he is whispering his value system into the princesses' ears: *Don't listen to*

God. You are your own god. Worship yourself; worship wisdom; worship beauty; worship wealth. Worship the scale. Worship the mirror. Worship your looks. And yet, these values leave us emptier than ever. They are beautiful lies: They look good on the surface, but on the interior, they are death to us.

What happens to a princess when her gaze is fixed on herself? She ends up hating what she sees because she is riddled with flaws. None of us can win the war against the mirror; it staunchly refuses to bend to our demands. We end up angry at our passing youth instead of focused on pouring our true beauty into the next generation of princesses. It's up to us to teach them the weight of their worth is the weight of their hearts; the palm of God, their only scale.

Out of the Furthest Darkness

Walt Disney was on to something profound. His fairy tales picture the longing for love in the heart of every princess and reveal how dedicated the enemy is to stealing her future. Whether it is the cruel witch, the wicked stepmother, or the evil fairy, the sinister figures in the fairy tales attempt to destroy the beauty, value, and purpose of the princesses. In *Snow White and the Seven Dwarves*, we see what happens when the evil queen is so focused on her image in the mirror that she turns against the beautiful princess.

"Slave in the magic mirror, Come from the farthest space!" the queen cries, the black wings of her cape arching behind her. "Through wind and darkness I summon thee: Speak!"

The mirror fills with flames.

"Let me see thy face!"

Through shadowy spirits, a mask emerges. "What wouldst thou know, my queen?"

"Magic mirror on the wall, who is the fairest one of all?"

"Famed is thy beauty, majesty," the mask says. "But hold, a lovely maid I see. Rags cannot hide her gentle grace. Alas, she is more fair than thee."

The queen's ghoulish eyes swell with fury. "Alas for her! Reveal her name!"

"Lips red as the rose. Hair black as ebony. Skin white as snow."

"Snow White?" she rages.

The mother carries the authority of the queen. She wears the crown, the purple gown, and oversees the land. But she is not just a queen with dominion over her people; she is a mother, positioned to help the princess grow into all that she can be.

But the Queen is the slave of the mirror. Coming from darkness, the mirror sucks her into its lies and turns her against her stepdaughter.

Infuriated that her daughter's youthful beauty surpasses her own, the Queen summons her huntsman. "Take her far into the forest. Find some secluded place where she can pick wildflowers. And there, my faithful huntsman, you will kill her!"

"But your majesty," he interjects. "The little princess!"

The huntsman knows well the value of the daughter. She is priceless, for she is to inherit the throne. And she is *good.* But the mother only sees the mask in the mirror. Gripped by jealousy, she demands he cut out the princess's heart.

But the huntsman cannot bear to kill the princess, so he tells Snow White to run and hide. She races in terror from the spirit of envy in her stepmother, wishing for a prince to save her.

What happens when the mother is so focused on herself that she cannot see the daughter? What happens when a generation of mothers enslaved by the mirror raises a generation of princesses? Do the daughters go off and running in search of a better future? Do they end up in the company of a bunch of dwarves (that is, fools)? Or do they wait for a prince to sweep them away and bring them all that their hearts desire? For sure.

This generation of mothers has had more surgical and esthetical "beauty" enhancements, augmentations, reductions, lifts, injections, treatments, and programs to improve their outward appearance than any before. And this generation of daughters has been more crippled by eating disorders, obesity, self-harm, sexually transmitted diseases, depression, and poor body image than any before. I fear that the mothers, fixated on the mask in the mirror, are in part responsible.

What would happen if we mothers turned away from the slave in the mirror, turned toward the faces of our daughters, and shifted their gaze to a mirror that never changes?

Is there really a mirror like that? A mirror that is satisfied? A mirror that reflects who we are and what we are worth?

Yes, there is.

4   The Second Truth:

You Are a Precious Creation

We are God's handiwork.

Ephesians 2:10

Barbie in the Kitchen

I look like I should be standing on top of a cake. I am wearing a soft pink gown, hoopskirt, and raspberry petticoats. My hair is piled high in a puffy bouffant. It is the thirty-fifth anniversary of the Barbie doll, and I am it, her, the doll beneath the get-up.

I don't know anything about girls and self-esteem. I've never weighed in on beauty and Barbie. I am only a woman in a makeup chair having my face transformed while I cry on the inside. I don't know where all the tears come from—I have yet to delve into the secret layers of my heart. I just know the tears are there.

Being Barbie is the seed from which my later passion grows. It is the seed of knowing what it's like to weep on the inside while wearing a smiling mask on the outside.

Years later, after I leave the modeling industry, I have this heart that becomes a little more tender each time I hear the story of a girl who doesn't feel like she's enough. The hurt wears a familiar face. I am acquainted with the longing, and I believe in the One who can heal it.

When I first heard the gospel while living in Munich, it felt like someone was feeding the empty belly of my ravished spirit with morsels of bread dipped in sweet wine. I savored the tang of grace and salivated for more. It tasted like truth. In small ways, I forgave my imperfections, even embraced them. I began to turn away from the mirror of the world to the mirror of God. My attention diverted from how I looked to how he looked and how he viewed me.

Leaving the modeling industry was no simple step. I had been building my career for 15 years, and turning away with no one's permission was one of the most courageous things I've ever done. At the same time, it was simple: I was leaving in pursuit of God's dreams for me, and his dreams seemed like a greater adventure with a greater destination.

Before I came home, my mother vacationed to Italy to see me and we went to the South. There we met a wrinkly Italian grandmother who reacquainted me with the real meaning of home. Little dogs scurried around her tiny house and a delectable aroma wafted from her kitchen.

The runways of Milan were worlds away. This woman grew sweet, juicy oranges and ruby red tomatoes in her backyard. Her chubby hands ground her own flour and her stumpy fingers pressed the *orchiette,* a thumb-shaped pasta signature to her town. She pureed rich tomato sauce from scratch, served hand-pressed golden olive oil from the farmer, and baked her own crusty bread. As I watched her stir the red sauce with a worn wooden spoon, a knowing stirred in me. I knew I had to return home, to my own mother and grandmother, to God, to family, and to the kitchen.

When my feet landed back in the United States, I came home to what I had known as a child—my mother cooking in the kitchen, making three square meals for her family. On Sundays, Mom baked flats of seasoned bone-in chicken until the whole kitchen filled with the scent of crisp brown skin and juices steaming in the pan. She made thick, cheesy, sausage-stuffed lasagna. Pea soup simmered all day with ham hock and thyme. She made gooey fudge brownies, carrot cake with cream cheese frosting, pumpkin bread, zucchini bread, banana bread galore. As a little girl I used to help her mix in the nuts, lick the bowl and spoon, and peek over the countertop at the steaming cakes.

It was the same in my husband's home. Shane's mother, Linda, is famous for her hospitality. On any given holiday she will decorate the table like sweet Jesus is coming for dinner. Her Thanksgivings are filled with perfectly whipped mashed potatoes, a sweet potato casserole with brown sugar-cinnamon pecans that is more like dessert than dinner, and a brined turkey so tender you'd be a fool not to slosh it in the rich giblet gravy. Aside from her delectable roasts, cakes, soups, and stuffings, there is nothing so sweet as Linda's famous chocolate pie, made from a recipe handed down from legendary Grandma Inez—a recipe that I am teaching my daughter.

As the women gather in Linda's kitchen, our words mingle like cups of flour, tablespoons of sugar, and pinches of salt, combining to make a new flavor. When times are confusing, we just stir the sauce and check the meat and make small talk. Sometimes we even foresee answered prayers when nothing points to them. Even in the most difficult times, we will cook a perfect roast, knowing blessings await on the other side of heaven.

When I was modeling, beating my body with starvation, overexercise, and denial became a way for me to put a big red punching bag on my fist and pound at whatever I wanted. But it wasn't an answer. I became too weak to fight and got pummeled when the stronger man entered the ring.

It is so clear to me now. When life isn't what you wish it would be, sometimes the best way to fight for what you want is to buck up and break out the garlic and oil, open the can of sauce, dice the tomatoes and onions, sauté the meat, and stir.

Sometimes, we just need to do what our mothers did: get in the kitchen.

A Fast from the Mirror

I look into the mirror and can hardly stand what I see. My skin, once creamy, soft, and pure, is riddled with sores. Pimples mar my forehead, cheekbones, and jawline and rear their blaring faces on either side of my mouth. They are cystic and vile, clustering in haphazard pocks. I hate these ugly sores. I hate looking at myself—and the more I do, the larger they get, the more they multiply, and the greater the intensity of the anxiety creeping down my neck.

I try peels and washes and medicine and treatments. I spend money on useless remedies that don't work. My skin only gets worse. We have just moved to a new town, and I can tell you right now I'm not signing up for Bunko or Bible study! I thought it was bad when I left the modeling industry ten years ago. Now it's a nightmare.

Mortified that these cysts have gathered in clusters around my jawline, I barely leave the house. As my husband walks through the door, I shrink back in shame and cover my face. The treatments have made it so dry on top of the sores that I can peel off my skin like a snake in flaky ribbons. The kids want to know "what is wrong with Mommy's face."

Under a black sky speckled by pinholes of light, I pound my fists on the backyard deck, begging God to heal me.

In a final plea for help, I drive hours to meet a famous dermatologist. Surely he will fix me; he will give me a magic prescription to make this torture go away.

He examines me closely. He notices not only my sores but the distress they are causing me. As I describe my experience, my face flushes and eyes fill with hot tears. I can barely catch my breath to speak.

"My dear," he says compassionately, "you are not an acne patient. You are a heart patient."

I lean closer to make sure he sees the rabid pimples so clearly ruining my face.

"Your issue originates not in the skin, but in the heart and mind," he says, as if teaching me a lesson. Ushering my attention to a diagram on the wall, he explains how the ventricles to the heart and the mind connect to the deepest layers of the skin. "You appear to have a belief in your heart and mind that you have to be perfect. Was something like that planted in you as a child?"

I start talking and I don't even know what comes out. I slobber all over my words and have to collect myself with tissue.

He considers anti-depressants but settles on a hormone therapy which will take until Easter to work. It's not even Thanksgiving yet.

I am panicked. My face is marred. I want a prescription to heal this now. Instead, he recommends counseling. "Once the emotional healing comes," he says, "the physical healing will follow."

He sends me across the hall to a kind and gentle esthetician. As I am lying on the gurney I'm hoping she will recommend a magic cream that will put a stop to this nonsense. She doesn't. Instead she tells me to stop looking in the mirror.

"Take a month off," she says with peaceful music playing in the background. "Do what you love; focus on what makes you happy. Don't look."

I cry half of the way home and start my fast from the mirror by the time I pull into the driveway.

When I get home, I announce that we will no longer focus on Mommy's skin. "I am more than my skin," I tell my children, and that is that. For forty days, I don't look.

About three weeks into the fast I am dropping my son off at preschool and see his teacher, Miss Jan. Miss Jan knows my story. She knows that I'm writing a book, getting counseling, and that the buried pain of the past has surfaced on my face. Jan is one of those people who naturally invites you to take off the mask, get real, and tell the truth. I love women like her.

"Jen!" she exclaims as I hang up Zach's backpack. "You look radiant! What have you been doing?"

What have I been doing? I have not looked in a mirror for 21 days; I have turned the rearview mirror in the car away from my eye line; I have not glanced at my reflection in store windows. I have woken up in the morning, popped in the contacts in dim lighting, and done what I love: read the Word and write. I have gone to Bunko and Bible study. I have laughed with my family and ignored how I looked. What have I been doing? I've been living, and I've forgotten what I look like.

The Bible says, "Those who look to him are radiant; their faces are never covered with shame" (Psalm 34:5). When Moses went up on the high mountain to go face-to-face with God, his countenance became so blazingly radiant that later, when he returned to the Israelites, he had to cover his face with a veil.

Something happened on my fast. I found out what I love and what makes me happy, and I didn't find that from looking in the mirror or gazing at myself. I found it from turning away from the bathroom mirror and looking into the one mirror that never changes. Aside from reading the Word night and day, I tromped the mountain trails and counted stars with my kids. I wrote my heart out. I finally told my story.

On one of the last days of my fast, I got a call from a girl in Georgia who saw my website and was looking for a speaker for a teen girls' event called "Unmasked."

She asked me if I thought I could speak on that topic.

"Sure," I said. "I can talk about what it is to be unmasked."

When the emotional healing came, the physical healing followed. I learned everything I know about beauty in the Word during that fast. It changed the way I saw beauty and changed the way I saw myself.

And then I came down from the mountain and spoke what I knew to be true.

The Creator Speaks

I look into the heart of my creation and weep, love and sorrow a crimson tide. I adore my children and the ways you are each different—fantastically, uniquely distinct.

You are the triumphant poem of my heart, each delightful word a note to a melody. You are a handcrafted vase, molded from a mound of clay. You are a brilliant tapestry with a dream stitched into the fabric of your heart.

You are curious children full of wonder, dedicated mommas with hopes and heartaches, teachers pouring into the next generation, writers who dream, dancers, singers, actors, ranch hands, athletes, businessmen, and world changers. You are all reflected in my eye. My people make up the kaleidoscope of who I am—together, you are the image of me.

Sorrow overflows, however, when I see my children squandering their wonderful bodies as if they are trash. It hurts me personally, and I want you to know it.

I hear the world saying, "It's your body; you can do whatever you want with it!" But I don't say that. Did you make your body? Did you fashion it with your hands and heart? Did you buy it from me? What price did you pay?

I paid the price. I spent everything I had on you in blood and tears. I received the stripes on my own flesh to buy back yours. I am your Maker and your body is my creation; a lot of work went into it. When I am chiseling a masterpiece, I am so proud of my design. In fact, I did a fine job on you, and I still am working. I want you to see it this way.

When you fixate on the mirror or the scale or the measuring tape, you might not realize that what you see is only a part of all you are. Did I not give you a destiny that cannot be seen in the mirror? A wish? A goal? A talent? A skill? A dream?

My daughter, turn to me for your value. Do not look to a mirror that is ever-shifting.

Some of my children spend their precious lives focused on feeding themselves instead of feeding the hungry, examining themselves instead of exacting solutions, and critiquing imperfections instead of perfecting others in love. They squander their gifts trying to please man or the mirror or both.

Why do you look up at me and question me about my children, question me about the work of my hands? Why do you say "He did not make me" and "He has no hands" when I held the knitting needles, when I crafted your dreams?

Do you think beauty is a woman who resembles a doll instead of a child with a chocolate-smeared smile looking up at the moon?

Do you think a man with a scalpel knows more of beauty than I who speckled the night with stars, who shook out the woolen blanket of the hills, who frosted the mountains with powdered sugar and forged a way for you to go down, crisp wind in your ears?

Do you think your frailties point to my failure?

Do I not know real beauty when I allow trees to shed their rust-colored leaves so children can crunch and play in them?

Do I not know real beauty when I give a man a lemon chiffon sunrise with a lavender horizon so he might hope for a better future?

Do I not splatter the sky night and day with my name: Creator?

When you see me face-to-face, you will see all. Now you see in part, a poor reflection as in a mirror, but then you will know fully as you are fully known.

The Baby Blanket

My mother knits. When I was pregnant with our first child, Olivia, Mom knit an intricately designed baby blanket for her. She used two spools of delicate yarn for each stitch, one of which was super fine with tiny little threads jutting every which way. She also used a variety of pastel colors to create a pattern of blocks in the blanket. Mom worked her fingers to the bone knitting that blanket, and when she gave it to me, it was soft and pretty and made with so much love.

But it wasn't perfect. The blocks hung a little lopsided when I held the blanket up in the light.

Over the years, I nursed Olivia in that blanket. I tucked her in at night in that blanket. And when she got older, she dragged the blanket through the house and up and down the stairs. That blanket bore a lot of mileage and now it's worn and dull, with holes in it. It's more lopsided than it ever was.

Would I ever tell my mother, "I'm sorry Mom, but that blanket isn't quite right. It's got so many flaws. I would have chosen different yarn, different colors, a different pattern. It's really not good enough for me, Mom, even though I know you worked really hard on it. Can you make a better one, without so many errors woven in?"

Of course I would never tell my mother that; I don't even believe that. But this is the attitude of far more women and girls than we know. We look up at God and say, "You could have knit me together with a D cup, you know! Why didn't you give me smaller thighs or a flatter stomach or better skin? I hate my hair! I want hers! Why can't I sing or dance or act? You should have done so many things differently! I'm very unsatisfied with your work, God."

He tells us we are fearfully and wonderfully made, and then we turn around and tell him it's not good enough, even that we hate his creation.

Of course the world's answer is to fix it from the outside in.

Extreme body makeover, baby. Slice up your body and rebuild it the way you want. Choosing to change the bodies we have been given is a personal decision that calls for a conversation between the potter and the pot. It's solely between God, a woman, and her husband, and it's not for others to judge.

Yet we should remember our bodies are not our possessions; they are God's and they are our husbands' and decisions regarding them are between us and them.

Some women are very open about their plastic surgery and make no apologies for it, saying they have "lived in this house for a long time and it's high time to fix it up." We just have to be aware that fixes to a house made of stone and mortar are different from fixes to a house made of blood and bones, because within the latter beats a living heart.

The heart is the key to all real beauty, and no external fixes can beautify the heart.

So the question we must ask ourselves is if we are caring not only for the body but for the soul. Are we only making over what people can see, or are we also beautifying the most important part—what people can't see? As *The Little Prince* puts it, "It is only with one's heart that one can see clearly. What is essential is invisible to the eye." [5]

Heaven's Exchange

The good news is, when we get to heaven we are not going to walk over to a rack of robes and have to choose a size 4 or 14. Saggy breasts or bulbous bellies or thick thighs will not be an issue. The only measurements we will perceive will be the grand stature of the kingdom. We will see Jesus face-to-face, we will walk with him in his grand creation, and we will gaze upon him at the center of the throne.

We will not long for a perfect body because perfection will be ours. There will be no more pain, no more disease, no imperfection, and no longing. Not only will we see all that is beautiful, but we will be united with it; we will bathe in it; we will be part of it. [6]

But for now we are on earth; we are in these tents called bodies, these cloaks of flesh. As I see it, we have three options:

Option 1: We can make our bodies an idol. We can worship our bodies, obsess over them, and idolize them as the central focus of our lives. We can devote the vast majority of our time and energy to controlling or perfecting the body. Obsessively, we can fix our eyes on the mirror, the scale, the measuring tape, the calories, our size and shape. But we must also be aware we might miss out on a life of real beauty if we choose this option.

Option 2: We can give up completely on the quest for beauty because we don't believe we'll ever reach it. We can eat whatever we want, become overweight, and get sick. We can dress sloppily and not care for ourselves, even though that's certainly not what our husbands signed up for or our children deserve.

Option 3: We can accept the truth of 2 Corinthians 4:16: "Though outwardly we are wasting away, yet inwardly we are being renewed day by day."

There are women who work out their whole lives and never seem to shed the weight they want to lose. It's hard to live in a body that cannot be controlled and will not bend to our demands. It's painful to live in a body which isn't measuring up to our expectations. But ultimately, it's up to the woman to reach out for the edge of his robe and believe that in one way or another, he will heal her. It's the woman's spirit which strengthens her to push through the crowd, speak the truth, and look to him to measure her value.

When we see ourselves as God sees us, we care for ourselves because we believe we are worth it. We have a responsibility to teach the younger generation to age well. We have to teach them that caring for our bodies well also means caring for our souls.

We can be the best we can be in the skin that we are in. If I do that and you do that and our mothers and grandmothers and daughters and girlfriends do that, we can make some real impact.

Finally, some of us need to meditate on our grandmothers. Humor me for a moment and imagine your grandmother in her underwear. Goodness, she looks old, doesn't she? The body is wasting away. The clock is ticking, and as it ticks, the body ages, no matter what we try to do to freeze time.

When my Grandma Betty died, she was 91. Like a tall candle long burned, the wax melted in clumpy threads, Grandma's whole body was dripping toward the floor. She suffered from osteoporosis and was melted over in a hump.

Every time I would go visit Grandma Betty, she would look through the peephole, swing open the door, and clap her hands in sheer delight. She was all lit up from the inside; her eyes were like sapphires on the sunlit sea, always sparkling. She had a beauty that shone from the inside out.

Grandma didn't grow up in a world where Botox or boob jobs were an option. She practiced standing up straight, took her calcium, ate her salmon and spinach, did water aerobics wearing a swim cap, and tried her best to keep track of her keys and glasses. She just never got old on the inside. All hunched over but still bright and beautiful, Grandma used to say to me, "You know, I am the same on the inside. I just look different." And in her eyes, I saw the reflection of a woman I'd like to be.

The day of our last visit, I was nine months pregnant with Olivia. Grandma was tired, so I lay on the bed with her and rubbed the tensed muscles around her tender spine until she drifted off to sleep. Two days later, I gave birth to Olivia just as Grandma Betty was admitted to the hospital. Downward she spiraled until she was put in a ward where they would not allow newborns. I visited her as soon as I could. She was unresponsive, her mouth hung open, and her eyes were in a far-off stare. They were no longer feeding her.

"I love you…I love you…" I cried into her ear.

"No one has gotten through to her," my uncle whispered.

But I wouldn't stop saying those words, my tears traveling through the creases in her face.

And then she heard me. She smiled. Her eyes winced and she cried too, our tears merging in a mixed stream. No one got any response from her after that.

She never got to hold Olivia in that baby blanket, or even see her.

But I knew it was heaven's exchange. From dust we came, to dust we return, and our spirits to God who made us.

I couldn't hold Grandma anymore, but I could hold my baby girl and see that God exchanges beauty for ashes, and it has nothing to do with what we see in the mirror.

Someday, I will see Grandma Betty again, and she will be renewed in glory. Maybe she'll be standing in the strawberry patch, or clipping roses, just the way I remember her as a little girl.

We are the precious creations of God, his craftsmanship, and only he can define beauty for us.

The Bible tells us to live by faith, not by sight; to fix our eyes not on what we can see, but on what we can't see—because what is seen is temporary, and what is unseen is eternal (2 Corinthians 4:18).

How did I get over my eating disorder? How did I move beyond my skin problems? I chose to stop fixing my gaze on myself; I turned my attention to God and his dreams for me. In the mirror of his Word, we see that he not only crafts our bodies, but he weaves a finely stitched thread through our hearts—the fiber of his love, which holds us together.

It is a beautiful lie to believe beauty is defined by what is visible. As he crafted the sea and everything in it, he filled us with depths of beauty that cannot be seen on the surface. It's our job to dive deep within the waters of our souls and ascertain the treasures embedded there. It's up to us to carry those jewels to the surface and bless the world with their value. It's up to us to believe we are more than the sum of our parts. We are filled with the capacity to reflect the image of our Creator, and through us, he continues to create, manifesting his wisdom, love, and power through these imperfect bodies of ours.

It's up to us to embrace the gorgeous truth: We are the precious creations of God. He is the potter; we are the clay, his unique design, and it's the jewels within us that make us shine.

5　The Third Lie:

You Are What Magazines Tell You

Magazines twist our notions of women's
worth; the devil is their partner.

666 Ways to Change You

8*12 Easy Ways to Look Great Right Now!* cries the magazine cover. Wow, I would love to look great right now, but I'm in an old gray sweatshirt and don't have a speck of makeup on. My sweats are three sizes too big and you'd have to pay me to put on a pair of slacks or even jeans. I haven't had time to do my hair and am lucky if I get the dishes and laundry done today.

Who has time to "look great right now"? Right now I need to pay the mortgage and pick up chicken for dinner and take my son to buy a birthday gift and get the car washed. Right now I need to answer fifty emails and scrub the dog stains on the carpet and make that pediatrician appointment! Right now? Can we look great later, please? And can it really be *easy*? Does it take 812 things? I don't have time for 812 things, especially right now.

Now that I think of it, I don't have time for 812 things later, either. Later I need to run three loads of laundry, clean up the dishes from breakfast, cook dinner, rake up the leaves, pay the bills, and go walking with my neighbor because putting the baby in the stroller is the only way to keep him from tearing apart the house. Later I will make sure I look decent enough to go to Target. Later, when the older kids get home, I will cook up snacks and help with home-work. And by the time my husband walks through the door, I will try to make myself and the house look as nice as is realistic at the moment. *Later.*

Bottom line, Ms. Magazine: I already have 812 things to do and looking good is only one of them.

I have a stack of classic magazine covers I have collected over the years. The number-one selling magazine in America, *Cosmopol-itan*, and its girlfriends, *Glamour* and *Vogue*, are totally focused on how good you look, how great the airbrushed models and actresses within their pages look, and how you can lure a man.

The world is riddled with starvation, disease, pain, and violence… but also miracles, salvation, healing, and massive amounts of love. The fashion magazines won't tell you any of this, though. They're totally focused on your appearance and your sexual satisfaction. Should those things be the main focus of our attention?

Let's flip through some of these magazines.

Here is just a sampling of the cover titles in my stack:

- Best of Beauty: 245 Winning Products For the Most Amazing Skin, Hair & Body
- Wrinkle Fighters, Hair Thickeners, Skin Calmers, Split-End Fixers, and More
- How to Get Fresh, Clear Skin; Glossy, Sexy Hair; Fast, Flattering Makeup; A Sleek, Smooth Body; and Bright, Flawless Nails; Plus How to Dress Thinner and Find the Perfect Jeans
- Sexy New Updos: Not One Bit Uptight

- Celebrity Hair Lust: Step-by-Step Tips
- Totally Gorgeous Skin: A Brighter, Fresher Face
- 300 Summer Dresses, Bags, Sandals, Sexy Heels
- 240+ Shoes, Bags, and New Looks
- 624 Ways to Get the Most out of Your Look
- 259 New Looks For Every Body and Budget
- 100 Party Hair & Makeup Ideas
- Your Best Body Ever! Raise Your Metabolism, Get Better Curves, Age-Proof Your Skin
- Perfect Swimsuits for Every Shape
- Sexy Summer Hair: Get Gorgeous Volume Fast
- Millionaire Hair: Thick, Shiny, Totally Luxurious
- Kick Your Butt! The Secret to the Best Behind Ever!
- A New Way to Perfect Skin
- Eyes Wide Open: The New Cosmetic Surgery
- Ageless Beauty!
- Perfect Hair and Gorgeous Glow!
- Beauty For Under $10!
- Look Amazing Without Makeup!
- The Makeover Issue! What Can You Really Change in 30 Days? A LOT! Fix Your Sex Life, Your Friendships, Your Booty!
- What Does Your LOOK Say About You? Ask Our Beauty Shrink!

Here are my two all-time favorites: "176 Tips to Simplify Your Life" (as if I need 176 more things to do to make my life simpler) and "Instant Happy!" If happiness were instant, we would have bought it a long time ago, Ms. Magazine.

Are these covers wrong? Not my call. Overwhelming? Assuredly.
Statistics say that girls see four to six *hundred* images from the media
every day, and after spending only one to three minutes perusing a
fashion magazine, 70 percent of us begin feeling guilty, depressed,
ashamed, and angry. The crazy thing is that women who read fitness magazines are twice as likely to use unhealthy dieting mecha-
nisms like purging and laxatives. Why would this be? Because they
are looking at unrealistic images they can never live up to. The average model is thinner than 98% of American women and at least a
quarter of the women in Miss America pageants and *Playboy* cen-
terfolds meet the criteria for anorexia.

According to *Teen* magazine, 35 percent of girls ages six to twelve
have been on at least one diet, and 81 percent of ten-year-olds are
afraid of becoming fat. Their minds have become so influenced by
the images of the media that they have an incorrect perception of a
healthy weight. Over half of teens say they want to lose weight. The
reason they cite: magazine pictures. The images as well as titles in
the magazines have a subtle way of shifting our focus off our gifts,
talents, and abilities, and onto the self. The more we gaze at these
unrealistic images of ideal beauty, the more we turn inward, feeling
less than beautiful ourselves.

I peer for five minutes at the images of the women on the covers of magazines and I, who used to be on the covers of magazines,
feel less than perfect. I could easily spiral into jealousy, depression,
and self-hatred if I looked too long at the airbrushed beauties with
their perfect skin, hair, and bodies. But I won't, because I know that
image isn't true to life. I knew models whose lives were riddled with
bulimia, sexual promiscuity, drug use, low self-esteem, purposeless-
ness, anger, starvation, loneliness, and more. Many of today's cover
models have undergone treatment for self-harm, addiction, and
abuse. All of their appearances have been altered by expert makeup
artists, lighting specialists, photographers, and of course the air-
brush. Most have personal trainers, dieticians, and plastic surgeons

and spend inordinate amounts of money on beauty treatments. We know this. But our daughters don't.

For them, the magazines are even more exhausting. On one *Seventeen* magazine cover, a less-than-stellar-example of a star has china white skin, bleached white hair, and shimmering blue eyes. On the cover of *Cosmogirl!*, that same star is tanned with auburn hair and green eyes. How are our daughters supposed to keep up? The titles are "875 Ways to Look Beautiful," "527 Ways to Shine for the Holidays," and "Flirting Moves Guys Find Irresistible."

Seventeen features "656 Fashion & Beauty Ideas: Look Pretty Now!" and "Kissing Secrets Guys Wish You Knew." The titles are plastered over an image of a star who is well known for her hard partying, nearly-naked fashion statements, and much-publicized dating violence. When our girls get out of school for summer, *Seventeen* will hand them "859 Ways to Get Pretty," tell them how to "Look HOT in a Bikini," and how to "Make Guys Worship You." When it's time for them to start school again, the same magazine will give them "825 Ways to Look Pretty," "Get Shiny Hair and Perfect Skin by the First Day of School," and tell them how to "Get Everything You Want This Year: Great Body, Tons of $$$, Amazing Clothes, and Mega Confidence!"

Our girls just don't have enough as it is, apparently. They have to do thousands of things to become pretty and when they do, they will have all their hearts desire.

And we haven't even opened the magazines yet.

Flawed and Fabulous

When I do open the magazines, this title jumps out at me: "Fabulous is Flawless." I guess I'm not fabulous then, because I am so *not* flawless.

Here's my reality: I have seven horizontal lines on my forehead and two vertical ones between my eyes and the money I could have spent on beauty treatments is going to be under the tree this year with a big bow on it for my kids. I used to be in Jordache ads in *Glamour* magazine; now you'd have to airbrush me to make those pages. My car is dirty and my cupboards are half full and my wardrobe is so outdated it's hilarious. I haven't worked out in months but I did last year…does that count? The breakfast dishes still aren't done, the dog poop still isn't picked up, the car still isn't washed, and my to-do list has been topped by another one. If fabulous is flawless, I'm not it.

But this is what I know: I am fabulous, with all my flaws, and so are you. There is not one page in one magazine on earth which has the power to define us.

What do real women want? Is it 565 ways to look good? We are so much deeper than that. Taking a list from the women I know: we want our husbands to long for us the way they did when we were dating. We want our kids with learning disabilities to find their identity in more than test scores. We want our children to be secure, to make it, and to pick themselves up when they fall. Some of us really want a way to refill those college funds we drained in the tough times; we need a financial plan or a better job. We long for reconciliation in our families. Healing in our relationships. Our best friends to come back to us. Our babies to be healthy and come home from the hospital for a very, very long time. Our in-laws to accept us and to honor our boundaries. The chemo not to hurt as much as it did last time. Our husbands to rise from their fall and live big again. We just want to know everything is going to be okay, even when it feels like it's not.

We want connection; we want forgiveness; we want freedom.

We are real women and we want the real stuff. We want what can't be bought or manufactured or airbrushed or marketed, and we know happiness isn't an instant formula. It's internal.

You and I are flawed…and fabulous. And deep down, we all want not thousands of things, but one thing: We all want to know, despite our frailties, that God will hear our desperate pleas and rain answers from the sky.

Cosmo Speaks

Cosmopolitan is the bestselling monthly magazine in the United States, with 64 worldwide editions. Over 100 million teens and young women in more than 100 nations read *Cosmo*. If we were to gather its readership into one locale, it would be the twelfth-largest country in the world.[7]

Oh, how *Cosmo* speaks!

On a sample of covers, we find these titles plastered over the body of an eighteen-year-old starlet who has battled eating disorders and cutting and endured rehab for a nervous breakdown: "SEX FUN FUN FUN: New Erotica; Mostly-Naked Men; Sex He Craves—Inside: A Bonus Edition So Hot, They Made Us Seal It." Are we aware the cover model is not even legally allowed to drink a glass of wine? She started out on *Barney and Friends*, then she was a Disney pop star, now she's a poster child for sex.

Are we brushing the edge of child pornography and calling it fashion? On another *Cosmo* cover the actress is seventeen, not yet out of high school, and written over her pubic bone is the title, "Too Naughty to Say Here—But Have You Tried This Sex Trick?"

Some of the most favored actresses in Hollywood are posing half-dressed on the cover of *Cosmo* with titles like "21 Naughty Sex Tips" and "Dirty Lying Brides" written on their bodies. Do these teen idols realize the message they are sending to 100 million high school and college girls who read these magazines? The message is this: your body is a toy and sex is a game. Have at it, girl! That's a pretty powerful message with some tough consequences for young women.

We can't blame the covergirls, although at this point they could boycott *Cosmo*, as some have. I myself was on a cover of a magazine in Australia and the editors wrote tacky titles over my shoulder that I would never have agreed to. I had no input on that; I didn't see the cover until the world did.

These magazines tell us we have the right to do whatever we want with our bodies and sexual "freedom" is actually freedom. But sexual freedom is enslavement. Sex outside of marriage, whether in the form of sleeping around, incest, adultery, or prostitution, can lead to such heartbreak and pain that all the pages in all the magazines in all the world could not put words to the despair.

To go even deeper, we have to realize it's not the magazines that are the problem. The printing press, after all, was originally invented to print Bibles. What did we do with it? We printed pornography. Our hearts are the problem.

We have to be savvy to the beautiful lies we see in the magazines. We have to be able to distinguish lies from truth and unhealthy messages from healthy ones. The main lies coming from the magazines are:

1. You are not enough the way you are.

2. You are the master of your body.

3. Your flesh is your value, but your flesh has no value.

But here's the deal: Women run these magazines. From the head editorial staff on down the list, *women* create the content, design, and message of the magazines. Women, not men, are telling other women and girls they have to change to be pretty enough; women are telling them that while their flesh is their value; ultimately, their flesh has no value. It's usable, reusable, and disposable.

I have personal experience with women promoting this message. My modeling agent in Hollywood was notorious for telling girls they had no chance of making it in the business because they were not tall enough, their jaws were not square enough, their figures were not proportionate enough, their lips were not plump enough, and their skin was not clear enough. And the women who ran the magazines in Europe could be all the more ruthless. With a whisk of their wands they could dismiss a girl as "average" or make her a star.

For all the men who attempted to take advantage of me, I'll never forget the *woman* who gave it her best shot. She was a publicly proclaimed lesbian who ran a world-famous magazine in Paris. In the quiet of her vast office she asked that I hike up my skirt on the guise that she wanted to see my inner thighs. At eighteen years old, I had to stop her at the panty line.

She clearly felt it was perfectly fine to manipulate a girl from small-town America standing alone in her office. She even left me with some odd words accompanied by a rude snort. "You might as well stop being a prude right now, sweetheart, because people will end up seeing it all anyway," she said, and sent me on my way.

From the chief editorial offices all the way to the girls lying around on their bedroom floors surrounded by fashion magazines, the messages are warping our minds. Instead of empowering us, they are making us feel and behave worse. This generation of girls has the worst self-image of any before it. Depression, eating disorders, and low self-worth are the most common mental health problems of girls today. We warn our daughters about the dangers of drugs, alcohol, and smoking, but do we warn them about the impact fashion and fitness magazines can have on their psyche? If looking at something makes a woman or girl feel guilty, depressed, and ashamed about her body, then she shouldn't be looking at it, period. And this comes from someone who was in the magazines. I'm coming out of the pages to whisper, "It's a lie."

You are more than your body.
You are more than your appearance.
You are more than enough.
You are loved. Precious. Holy.
You are beautiful just the way you are—right now.

Battle Cry

I'm not sure why they started showing up in my mailbox. I didn't order them. I wouldn't in a million years have subscribed to them. But there they were: *Glamour, Cosmopolitan, Allure.* Month after month, I disputed the charges on my account. Month after month, they kept arriving.

So now I have a high stack of magazines with torn pages, articles ripped out and highlighted, and images analyzed and scattered all over my desk and floor.

Within the magazines, I find blatant lies.

Your body is your value.

You have no value.

Your body is a toy. Sex is a game. Have at it, baby girl.

Within these pages are a plethora of ideas on how girls can tear their hearts into little pieces. These magazines give girls step-by-step instructions, diagrams, and endless tips on how to please their "partner" or themselves. The articles and advertisements even have the gall to promise girls that sexually pleasing their "guy" will turn him into Prince Charming: he will take them on candlelight dinners, listen attentively, and be smiling for days. The girls are told to keep their options open. If one guy doesn't work out, they can move on to another "partner," gender non-specific, and try some new tricks.

These magazines are not marketed to married women. Married women read *Cooking Light*. Married women are flipping through the pages of *Good Housekeeping, Real Simple,* and *House Beautiful* in hopes of finding another way to cook chicken, organize the kids' closets, or hang drapes. Married women are researching the best health care for their kids, weighing private or public school dilemmas, seeking financial help, and keeping their eyes out for decorating, home, and health tips. Hopefully married women are investing time, energy, and heart into their marriage beds, staying fashionably dressed, working out, and eating healthfully. But let's get real: *Glamour, Allure,* and *Cosmo* are marketed to unmarried women and girls in their teens and twenties.

When girls leave college and want to enter into a lifelong committed relationship, I wonder how those tricks work out for them. When they walk away from college carrying the weight of their abortions, sexually transmitted diseases, torn relationships, shame, anger, betrayal, and hearts teeming with regret, then what? Is *Cosmo* going to help them heal?

This is how the magazines lie: Our bodies are sources of approval. Our bodies are a way to get the love we long for. Our bodies are ours. Sex is a ploy for man's attention. Sex is an activity, not a union. A game, not a communion. Sex is not something to bond husband and wife and bear children; it's about pleasing the self and others to earn love. As if love can be earned. The fact that *Cosmo* is the best-selling monthly magazine in the United States tells us a lot about the state of women's hearts. While we are looking for more ways to toss our bodies at whomever we please, the world is capturing God's girls, torturing them, and binding them to sexual slavery. An estimated three million women and girls are being bought, sold, and forced to sell their bodies for sex. I bet they would give anything for 100 million *Cosmo* readers to raise their voices in a battle cry for them.

What if we all stood together and cried, "Not me! Not you! Not her! No more! We are not just things. We are not just flesh. Our bodies are valuable and sacred and worth saving!"

Together, our voices can speak the real meaning of freedom. This isn't just a battle cry for women and girls. It's for the men too. Our future husbands deserve it; our sons, even more.

Protected

College girls in America may not be captured and forced to have sex, but most are choosing to give themselves away for free. Who pays the price? They do. According to Dr. Miriam Grossman, a campus psychiatrist and author of the astounding book *Unprotected*, campus counseling offices don't advise self-restraint; they advise latex.[8] Condoms, despite their failure rate, Grossman says, are "endlessly enshrined."[9]

This brilliant, concerned, faith-filled psychiatrist bemoans how political correctness in her profession endangers students. On college campuses, she says, "Infection with one of the sexually transmitted viruses is a rite of passage. It comes with the territory. Abortion is the removal of unwanted tissue, sort of like a tonsillectomy...

Students have gender-free 'partners': what difference does it make if they are male or female?" she asks, describing the mindset of campus counseling centers. [10]

According to Grossman, most campus counselors ignore the statistics which show practicing a life of faith is beneficial to a person's psyche. The counselors are taught to ignore the truth that sex outside of marriage causes heartbreak, shame, and an inability to concentrate on their schoolwork due to the simple fact that the girls are still attached to the boys who they had sex with.

Here is just one example of Dr. Grossman's patients, an eighteen-year-old girl who came to the college campus counseling center for depression and a relapse of bulimia. This girl, vomiting up to six times a day, said the end of a romance was the source of her pain. During their first meeting, the girl described to Dr. Grossman the short-lived relationship, her first experience with intimacy:

> "When it ended, it hurt so much," she said, weeping. "I think about him all the time, and I haven't been going to one of my classes, because he'll be there, and I can't handle seeing him. I was so unprepared for this... Why, Doctor," she asked, "why do they tell you how to protect your body—from herpes and pregnancy—but they don't tell you what it does to your *heart*?" [11]

Grossman says students are inundated with information about contraception, a healthy diet, the dangers of smoking, the importance of sleep, ways to cope with stress and pressure...but not a word about the havoc that casual sex plays on a young woman's emotions. College campuses produce pamphlets that say HPV is "normal" and can be treated instead of warning girls to guard their hearts.

Why are so many girls broken? And why are campus counseling centers ushering in "truckloads of antidepressants" to keep them functioning? Because many college counselors believe the lie. It's not only *Cosmo* and it's not just the girls. It's the politically correct culture that says it's okay to give your body away. Just protect yourself. Just use safe sex.

Try telling a girl whose heart was ripped by abortion or date rape or abandonment that sex is safe. Try telling a girl with HPV who is filled with shame, anger, and regret that sex is safe. Try telling me. You won't get it past me.

A condom can't protect your heart. A birth control pill can't delete the soul tie sex creates. A diaphragm can't heal a uterus riddled with sores. And an abortion can't rid the world of a child whose life is eternal. These are the truths they should be preaching on college campuses.

But if they don't, I will! Why? Because I really care about these girls.

Our bodies are not convenience stores where boys or men can come in and take what they want and leave us dirty and littered, the floor of our souls matted with sticky footprints and grime.

Our bodies should have guards standing out front because within us lies great treasure and worth, purpose and potential. Our bodies are worth protecting; our futures are worth preserving.

If you have a daughter or a niece or a neighbor or a babysitter who might be brainwashed by political correctness, speak up! Don't let *Cosmo* or the culture tell her what "safe sex" is. Let her know that safe sex is something which happens within safe boundaries—marriage—and where the covenant of God is fully explored and enjoyed. Healthy sex within marriage is a poem, a salve, a bond, and a blast.

Explain to her that sex makes you "one flesh" with a man and ties your soul to him. But if you are not married to him, this soul tie isn't enough to keep him with you. He's free to leave. He could desert you, leaving you with a broken heart.

Explain to her that the guy may not know how to heal her bleeding heart. He may not be a prince equipped to slay the dragon of her potential abortion; its fiery breath could scar her for life. Explain to her that most college boys aren't ready to raise babies and have no horse-drawn carriage set to go to the castle. The average sexually active college boy could easily be carrying AIDS or other sexually transmitted diseases that can shorten both their lives and prevent her from bearing children later on.

There are lifelong consequences to believing the beautiful lies of the culture. The cover girls look pretty. The titles sound great. But just because something looks good doesn't mean it is good. The articles appear attractive and certainly the photos maintain the image of perfection, but who is the god who worships outward beauty and twists women's internal worth? The devil is a good liar.

A Man's Worth

All this talk about women's worth has me thinking. What about a man's worth? Is he really just a boy toy as the fashion magazines present him? Or is he also made for more?

In my life, I want to see my husband lifted high. I want him to be all that he can be, and I want all of his dreams to come true. Part of him becoming all that he can be is knowing he can trust in his wife, knowing I've got his back and I would lay down my sword so he could wield his. Part of being a wife is giving yourself mind, body, and soul to your husband.

What the fashion magazines are promoting is not just that women are worthless, but their future husbands are too. Their future husbands—the fathers of their children—are not respected. Respecting our husbands means saving what is precious just for them. It is believing that not only are we worth the wait, but they are too. They are worth us saving our virginity. They are worth us preserving our bodies and caring for them like temples and not convenience stores.

A good man is a treasure. We would do well to teach our daughters to begin treasuring their future husbands now so they don't carry a load of soiled and grimy stones in their hearts when they walk down the altar.

A Better Headline

It's time for a better headline. It's time for women to stand up and use their voices to speak truth. The links between sexual impurity and drug problems, eating disorders, self-loathing, suicidal tendencies, alcohol abuse, broken marriages, broken hearts, and broken dreams aren't spelled out in the pages of *Seventeen, Glamour, Allure,* and *Cosmo,* but I've seen the influence of the beautiful lies written on the faces of women and girls. I've looked into their eyes and seen the damage to their hearts. I've read their long, pained letters and held their quivering hands. I've listened to the stories of grown women whose eyes are a well of regret and wrapped my arms around the delicate shoulders of weeping girls.

If only the magazines told *their* stories and spelled out *their* voices.

"I Don't Feel Beautiful Enough" could be the lead article. We could tell them what true beauty is. "Why Does My Heart Hurt Even When My Makeup Looks Perfect?" The article can tell them why.

I can see the titles of the articles I would publish: "Warning! Casual Sex Shouldn't Be Taken Casually! Inside, a Ten-Step Guide to Heal Your Heart." "Beware! Sex Leads to Pregnancy, Abortion, Heartbreak, and Disease." "12 Ways Sex Outside of Marriage Can Hurt You." "Newsflash: You Too Can Reach for the Healer!" "Your Husband Is Worth Waiting for and So Are You!" "You Are Loved! Beautiful! Holy! Holy! Holy! Receive Your God-Given Identity *Right Now!*"

6   The Third Truth:

You Are a Beautiful Temple

*We want to be united with the beauty we see, to pass into it,
to receive it into ourselves, to bathe in it, to become part of it.*

C.S. LEWIS, *THE WEIGHT OF GLORY*

Awesome

My head is heavy. My eyes burn. I put the baby down for a nap, intending to go upstairs and work on the talk for my next women's retreat, entitled "Bliss."

Bliss. Supreme happiness. Profound satisfaction. The joy of heaven.

But fatigue gets the best of me and I sense the Lord telling me to just lay my head down for a few moments to rest.

I drift to the couch. My cheek rests against the pillow; my eyes shut. I feel such utter relief. Every muscle in my body sinks into a dreamlike state.

Immediately, I am ushered into a giant meadow, so vast, so grand, so fertile, and so glorious it makes my heart swell and throb. Walking toward me is Jesus. Larger than life, he lifts me to his shoulders and carries me through the meadow. It is such a beautiful feeling. I am so supported, so held, so loved, and he carries me so I can see the endless view. There are mountains and woods in the distance; it is *bliss*.

He calls me by name. "Jen," he says, "Do you want to go to the temple?" I can tell he's excited for me to see it.

"Oh yes, Lord! Yes," I say. I get so excited when I am in God's house.

He takes me there on his shoulders.

When we arrive, I look around at the throng of people, masses of them, all facing him at the center, their hands raised, singing, "Holy."

It's crazy, I know, but I can't leave this part out. He looks me square in the eye, winks, and smiles as if to say, "Isn't it awesome?"

It is *awesome*! I join their worship, raising my hands. We, the people, are the precious stones that make up the floor of the temple.

And he is all we need.

The Lord Speaks

Magazines are made of words and images printed on paper, which burns in the fire. The only everlasting Word on earth was, is, and always will be the Word of God. The magazines have had their time of power and influence; I have allowed that. Yet like the glory of man, they will fade and fall.

Meanwhile my Word stands forever.

I'm very specific when I craft a temple: the measurements, the height, the adornments. I've crafted you the same way, because your body is my temple. The exactness, the artistry, the creativity—they are all reflections of my love for you.

But what if you came into my temple, with all its golden adornments, its burning candles and incense, the symphony of harps, drums, bass, horns, and piano, and inside you saw me selling wares at too high a price, ripping people off? What if you were drawn into the intricate carvings of angels on the marble façade but, on a closer look, found intravenous drugs, wicked incest, prostitution? What if I allowed hatred, bloody violence, and children to be whipped inside my house?

Where would you go then for peace and tranquility?

So it is with this generation of women. You don't know what a temple is! You don't know about my holy place! You don't know how it tears my heart to see my daughters sell themselves—or even worse, give themselves away for free.

It makes me cry.

I'm calling you back. I'm calling back my daughter, my temple, cleansed of her bloodstains, made pure as snow. Through the torn curtain, enter my chamber. Come away with me and learn how much you're worth, how sacred you are. Oh, how I love the temple.

Holy Ground

Despite what the magazines say about you, we find out who we are and what our value is in the reflection of who God is. What happens when we turn away from the multitude of voices we hear from the world and tune our ears to the Word? In the pages of that Word, we find that we are loved. We are cherished. We are precious. We are holy.

As we allow the truth of the Word to enter in, we can also discern the lies, contradictions, and confusion of the magazines. I can flip through a magazine and distinguish truth from lies, and I will teach my daughter to do the same. Together, we see that on one page, the magazine encourages us to "feel good" about ourselves, and on the next, we see an image that has been airbrushed to the point of perfection which no woman or girl can attain. Subliminally, this leaves us bothered and believing we are not enough the way we are. In one article it's okay to have sex without lasting commitment; in another it's important to take care of your "lady parts." These are conflicting messages.

God is not confusing like that. He says one thing about our bodies: they are holy. "Do you not know your bodies are temples of the

Holy Spirit, who is in you, whom you have received from God? You are not your own; you were bought at a price. Therefore honor God with your body" (1 Corinthians 6:19-20). And there's more: "Don't you know that you yourselves are God's temple and that God's Spirit dwells in your midst? If anyone destroys God's temple, God will destroy that person; for God's temple is sacred, and you together are that temple" (1 Corinthians 3:16-17).

God takes his temple seriously. He says we are the temple, the house for his Spirit, and he is more passionate about his house than anything else.

If you take a look at Old Testament temples, you will see they were beautifully adorned on the outside. Inside, they were inlaid with gold and precious stones. People literally had to take their shoes off to enter in, because entering the temple meant walking on holy ground.

So it is with our bodies. Our bodies are not things to be bought and sold, given away at will. Our bodies are also not objects to be analyzed and criticized. Our bodies are tents for his Spirit to dwell and reign in, if we allow him that place in our lives.

Throughout our lives, we have the option to choose sin over him. He lets us choose. Too often, we choose the way of self over the way of heaven. We choose binging over health. We choose many lovers over the devoted groom. We choose drugs over the banquet. We choose pornography over the sacred union. We choose hatred over love. We choose sin over what God wants for us.

Then we feel this darkness creep in and start to reign.

We run to the temple and cry, "Lord, Lord!"

And he says to us, "Please, don't just call me Lord. Let me *be* your Lord."

We all know what it feels like to not sense God with us, let alone within us. We have taken care to wear the mask, to make the outside as pretty as we can, but on the inside we are full of dead men's bones.

The Burning

It was right after we moved from California to Texas when I spoke at Deborah's luncheon. The room was filled with Christian businesswomen as I shared my story and spoke about the lies of the magazines. As I read the titles on the covers and tossed them to the ground with utter disregard, anger rose up and boomed through the microphone, though I did not realize it at the time.

For years I had been telling my story to audiences small and large, and it seemed that no matter how proper the environment, I shed a tear at one point or another. Yet that day it was not just one or two tears I could easily wipe away; this time they streamed down my face.

A few months later, Deborah invited me to lunch, and told me that I was still speaking as a victim of the world instead of a victor.

"You are still angry," she said.

"I *am* angry!" I cried in the corner booth. But why? What hurt was I still carrying after all these years?

She told me to open my heart every day and ask the Lord to "reveal any unclean thing within me."

I began to pray exactly that.

Then Shane found the pictures.

I was out of town when it happened. Shane was searching for pictures of the kids when they were little, thumbing through the boxes of photos stacked on my office shelves, hoping to make a collage of pictures for me for Mother's Day. He happened over a box of photos I should have long ago destroyed.

There he saw pictures taken fifteen years prior that ripped his heart in two. "She has been keeping these?! These are in my *home*? Why would she hold on to these? What else is there?" he questioned.

The bin of my modeling photos was right there at the floor of the closet. He ventured in. At the bottom of the bin he found photos that I wasn't proud of; photos that were not pornographic, but that positioned me as an object rather than as someone's future wife.

The titles on the photos were foreign, and he quickly did an online search to translate them: "Evil Spirit" was the headline across these pictures taken when I was only 18. Behind these photos were stories I had been too ashamed to tell.

It was less what was in the pictures and more how the photographer treated me behind the camera that hurt me most. These images represented the loss of my childhood, the loss of my values, as well as the way the industry manipulates young women.

What hurts us sometimes hurts our husbands even more, and that was certainly the case this day. Heartbroken and devastated, Shane's passion for his house consumed him. But he fell to the right place—his knees—surrendering his wife to God in a greater way than ever.

I came home and we celebrated Mother's Day. I had no idea the hurt and betrayal he felt in his heart, until the next morning he sent the kids to his parents' house and sat me down to talk.

The pain in his eyes was as real as the joy I had seen there so many times. The hurt was bigger than the room—it felt like it filled the whole world. Nevertheless, he calmly explained that today would be the day to clean out the closet.

"Every single photo that does not honor God, me, you, or our children, I want out of this house," he stated with kingly strength. Taking dominion over the property rightfully his, he spoke with authority: "Anything that compromised you will be burned in the fire. Not recycled. Not thrown in the trash. Turned to ashes.

"Right now."

Pulling all of the photos out of the portfolios and going through the stacks was an exhausting, confusing, and painful experience.

Every time I had tried to sort through the pictures over the years, I could never finish organizing them. Giving up, I would shut the bin and put it back in the closet.

Often the photos were all right on the surface, but I could only see the man behind the camera who had attempted to take me to bed after the shoot. As a young woman I would pose for the cover of a decent magazine, but sometimes the client or photographer—twice my age or older—would proposition me. The thought of it scared and disgusted me, and on multiple occasions I found myself running from these men, their predator spirits ever drawn to me.

When I came home from quitting the business, the images in the closet represented lies to me; I wanted to burn them all but didn't have the wisdom or courage to sort through them. Now, looking through them, my heart swelled with pain and anger clogged my throat. I was so young! So naïve! Why had I held onto the images of the men who forsook me? Why did I still carry my hurt from house to house? I never had the courage to look each person involved square in the face and say, "This is what happened, this is how you hurt me, and I forgive you."

It's much easier to put the hurt at the bottom of a box and try to forget it ever existed. But to forgive, you have to look the offender and the offense straight in the eye. Hurt, lies, and bitterness always surface. But we are the temple, and God will have no unclean thing in his house.

Something magical happened that night while Shane and I were alone in my office, sorting through the piles. God moved through him to help me do what I could never do: divide the good from the bad. Not all of my pictures represented painful times. Many didn't. Many were great adventures in beautiful places. Many were completely innocent. Most were taken with decent people. Many of the photos also represented my journey from a young girl into the world of modeling and into the world at large. It was my journey, and it wasn't all bad.

With hundreds of photos scattered all over the floor, I was finally able to look at each one and weigh its worth. Had this been a negative experience? Was I demeaned? Or was this a good experience? I sorted the images into "keep" and "burn" piles.

Late in the night we stood in the backyard under a starry sky. Shane took a big metal canister and we filled it with the pile of photos. Wearing a purple silk scarf over my head, I rested beneath my husband's wing and the cloak of the starry sky; my spirit knew the Lord had surfaced the evil thing in my life, and I had to face it and purge it.

Holding a large stick in his hand, Shane prayed as he stirred the burning images, poking at the hundreds of pages as they disintegrated into ash. In the hot orange flames I saw dead spirits crackle and groan. No longer would lies be my master; no longer would men be allowed to steal my identity. No more would their abuse live in my home or even in my heart.

That night, my shame became a bucket of ashes.

The burning changed things for us. For Shane, I became his radiant bride again. He said he saw me through the eyes of Christ: holy, without blemish, pure as the driven snow.

The fire purified me; I felt brand new.

Beauty from Ashes

We all carry unhealed wounds from house to house and city to city. We all wake up one day and realize we've believed a lie or have a secret unearthed that we wish would have stayed buried. We all know we've been forgiven but we have this insatiable desire to choke the life out of those who hurt us.

Yet the unforgiveness isn't choking the life out of our offenders; it's strangling us instead. Our spirits can't be free because we are holding somebody else in prison. My anger against people in my life didn't really hold them captive; it held me.

The burning was the beginning of the *real* forgiveness that had to take place. I couldn't just say of the men, "I forgive them" and sweep my hand across the sky and forget. I had to look each hurt in the face and say, "I forgive him or her for _____." I had to march each one to the cross. And all the while, I had to face my own sin and the choices I had made. I had to face both the foolishness and the ugliness in my own heart and take responsibility for my actions.

It started with the burning, but it was a long road to forgiveness. God was cleaning out my temple, turning over every unclean stone at the floor of my heart and washing me from the inside out. This cleansing tide went on for three long years. Sometimes I felt like I was never going to come up for air.

It was horrible and heavenly at the same time, but so worth the climb. And from that season, we birthed Samuel.

Baby Sam toddles toward me, holding the running hose in his chubby hand. His cherub face reflects the sunlight, beads of water dripping down his cheek. He splashes himself, gasping at the cold water. Smiling, he squints up at the bright sky, then turns and waddles away on the lawn; I feel like beauty is brushing past me.

As I bathe him in the kitchen sink, my hands soap his slippery skin. I feel his fragility, his tenderness, his sweet heart.

Like I do with our first two children, I remember when I first saw him fresh out of the womb. The love was so big it enveloped the entire room. I know how fast this goes. I can't lift our older son anymore. He's too big. So I linger a moment in the rocker, wrapping Samuel in his denim blue blanket; I squeeze him one more time before I lay him in the crib.

Maybe an atheist could look Samuel square in the eye and say he's not God's house; he's just a bunch of atoms and molecules or tissue, but I can't. I won't.

Children are a temple too.

I watch him shuffle after Shane as he mows the lawn, kicking the leaves, and I look up at the bright sky and say to my Lord, "You always bring beauty from the ashes."

Mary Speaks

Jesus loves the temple.

When he was a baby, Joseph and I carried him to the temple in Jerusalem to be dedicated, as was our tradition.

Then, when he was twelve, on our way back from the Passover feast, we lost him. For three days, we lost him! As a mother, I hope that brings you comfort! I was the mother of the Savior of the world, and I couldn't find him for three long days.

Where was he? We found him in the temple, of course: sitting there, listening to the teachers, asking questions, cool as a breeze.

Jesus called the temple his Father's house. It was the place he felt he most belonged. In his Father's house, the prophets spoke of the sword that would pierce my soul. In his Father's house, people were amazed at his understanding.

When I heard he had stood up in the temple and read from the scroll of Isaiah, revealing his purpose, I knew the wave of his identity would crash on the shore, cleansing some and drowning others.

Jesus went every day to his Father's house.

One day he made a whip of cords and drove out cattle and turned over tables.

"Zeal for my Father's house consumes me!" he cried, his passion so thick everyone could taste it in the air.

What was it like knowing he felt more comfortable in his Father's house than in mine? What was it like knowing he was my son, but God's Son, Savior, Lord, Messiah? I held his identity like treasure in my heart, sister. I embraced what I knew like one might squeeze a pillow close to her chest; I held my truth close.

He taught the people in the temple, he healed the people in the temple, and then he was beaten in the temple, in his Father's house. When they put the crown of thorns on him and mocked him, my soul could hardly bear the grief. Every tear in his flesh tore my heart. Every beating hit me in the chest. Every stripe scarred my soul.

When he spoke of his body being broken, I had no idea he meant what he said, that he was the temple. When he breathed his last breath on the cross, the curtain of the temple ripped from top to bottom. My heart ripped with it. I was so tired by then, the life sapped from my frame.

But when he rose I knew: I was the Father's house now, and his Spirit lived in me. I carried him not as a weight, but as a vessel. Zeal for the Father's house consumed me also.

Life wasn't just about worshipping God and caring for my family; life became about building God's house with my Son.

Now, here I am, in the temple with him, and he is still at the center.

I knew the Lord was holy, and I knew my body was a temple through which he could shine a light. But he did not force himself on me; I agreed to it.

When a child comes at an inconvenient time, when there is shame or derision over that child, when you are afraid and feel misunderstood, when you are alone and faithless, or when you doubt for one minute that an imperfect girl could be a holy vessel, think of me. People think I was the holy one—no, it wasn't that way. I just saw who I was in the reflection of who he was.

I opened myself up to his Spirit. He filled me as a temple and I birthed hope.

So can you, my sister! So can you!

My Father's House

Many of us might think, "I'm not Mary, okay? I'm not holy— I'm anything but. I have spent my days and nights soiling my temple from top to bottom, and there is no hope for me. I can't approach him. I'm too dirty, I had an abortion, I was sexually abused, I was stripping, I was in adultery, I have tortured myself, I have desecrated the temple. I'm *not* holy."

This is where the good news sweeps in and sweeps us out, clearing our temples of the unclean things, his light chasing out the darkness as truth rushes in. He says, "Your body is a temple," period. He says, "You are the temple," period. He says, "You are holy."

When we first ask Christ into our lives, it's like he is born into our "temples." At that point, he's just in the gate. Then, as we care for him, Christ starts to grow in us. He starts asking questions, listening to our answers, taking the temperature, just like he did in the temple when he was twelve. *What do you think of this?* he might ask. *How do you feel about that? What do you think God thinks about it?* If we listen well, we may be amazed at his answers.

Then one day Jesus stands up in us, as he stood up for the first time in the temple. *I came to bring you good news*, he says. *Why are you still behind bars when I came to free you? Why are you still wearing that outfit of despair when I came to dress you in a garment of praise? Why are you still wallowing in your ashes when I came to bestow on you a crown of beauty?*

Jesus might decide that we need a good temple-clearing. He just might come into our temples with a whip of cords and start driving out the sin. He might turn over the tables, shed a spotlight on some unclean thing in us, and say, *You can't live this way anymore. You are my Father's house, and zeal for you consumes me! I love you too much to let you keep living in anger, immorality, bitterness, selfishness, and lies. Even if it's going to hurt, I am going to drive this sin out of you and I will not give up until you—my house—are clean. Because I don't just want you to call me Lord; I want to be your Lord. I want to reign in the temple of you.*

The Temple Gate Called Beautiful

"They are so beautiful," I thought to myself as I laid my tired head on my husband's lap and gazed at the TV screen. He stroked my frizzy, kinky hair in silence. Back then he didn't have a clue about the battle raging in this fragile head of mine.

It was the Oscars, and the pretty people had come out to receive their applause. The hems of their long, flowing gowns swished as they sashayed down the red carpet, their glittering figures oh-so-sensuous yet oh-so-slight. They twirled and smiled over their shoulders in timeless poses for the camera, lingering so we could admire the line of their dresses. The exquisite fabrics hugged their curves as if they had just stepped out of a dream.

What is beautiful to you, God? I begged to know.

Then one day I came across the story of Peter healing a lame beggar in Acts 3:1-10. In the story, Peter and John are on their way to a prayer meeting when they see a man begging in front of the temple. The man, lame from birth, is forty years old, and every day, people carry him to the temple gate called Beautiful so he can beg. When he sees Peter and John, he puts out his cup, expecting to get something from them. But Peter and John look past the cup and directly at him. They tell him to look straight at them; they want to go face-to-face.

Likewise, the people I met in Germany in the park weren't too busy to look at a forlorn girl. They were kind of funny-looking, to be truthful—you wouldn't see them on any red carpet. But they stopped for me and didn't just flip a coin into my empty cup. They gave me water that would fill it forever.

Peter says to the beggar, "Silver and gold I do not have, but what I do have I give you. In the name of Jesus Christ of Nazareth, walk." Then Peter reaches out his hand and helps the beggar to his feet.

I love that, and I think God loves it too. Not only do they stop and look at him and offer him healing, but they touch him. They reach out their hands and help him get up. After a lifetime of paralysis the man's feet and ankles become strong and he jumps to his feet, praising God. Holding on to Peter and John, he goes into the temple courts, proclaiming the miracle. Everyone recognizes the beggar and the whole thing causes quite a ruckus.

I was once the beggar at the temple gate. Now I'm jumping around in the temple courts, proclaiming a miracle, causing a ruckus.

It wasn't my goodness or worthiness that healed me. It was Jesus, and it took someone looking into my eyes and offering me the power that strengthened my ankles and make me stand tall again.

Jesus is the gate. You are the temple. His Spirit within you is beautiful. Don't be in such a rush you can't see the beggar at your feet. Stop for him, look directly at him, give him what you've got. Reach out and help him up.

Be who you are made to be—a temple gate called Beautiful.

Refined by Fire

When it feels like God is turning over all your tables and rede-signing the interior temple of you, keep the gate open. Let the good in; keep the bad out. Build strong gates, but not so strong that Jesus can't come in and out freely and keep his temple clean. He longs to have access to the inner chamber of your heart where all transfor-mation happens by his Spirit. Let him in the inner room; he built it for himself to begin with.

If he reveals any unclean thing in you, agree with him to purge it. He really does want to make us more like him, and sometimes that takes refining like gold in the fire. The more we've been puri-fied, the more we shine. Like the gold, pure as glass, that Solomon laid in the floor of the temple, we too are priceless. It's the gorgeous truth—you are priceless to God. Let him be the Lord of the temple of you. Let him reign.

He knows how to beautify a temple. It's his expertise, and he likes to do it inside-out.

7   The Fourth Lie:

You Are the Mask You Wear

I used to love masks; now I prefer them shattered.

The Masquerade

As a kid I loved masks. I had this great collection of porcelain masks hanging on my bedroom wall. I loved their shiny façades, their mysterious eyes, their flawless faces. My friends thought the masks were freaky with their hollow, staring eyes, but I liked them, especially the porcelain one of Marilyn Monroe.

What was it about Marilyn Monroe that drew people to her? Was it her voluptuous figure, her captivating smile, her magnetic allure? Or was our desire for her all of these elements combined with her mystery? Beneath her shell, she was a human being, suffering, longing for love, perhaps lost. When her mask shattered, she fell with it, and her light extinguished before the world wanted it to. Regardless of the sad truth behind her fantastic smile, Marilyn's iconic beauty was put on a pedestal as the ideal image of womanhood in her day.

When I was a child, I also adored Michael Jackson. I read every available biography about him and tacked his posters on my bedroom walls. I kept scrapbooks of all the magazine articles written about him. Michael was the self-proclaimed king of pop, the best of the best—but again, lonely, vulnerable, afraid, and perhaps lost.

I cared so much about his childhood loneliness that I wrote him letters, telling him I could be a friend to him, someone to walk with him under the stars and be a listening ear. I truly was that idealistic. When I didn't hear back from him, I resolved to watch his life from a distance.

The theme of Michael's story, then and now, is that despite his fame, his soul suffered. His inner torment manifested itself publicly in his failed efforts to achieve what he thought was the perfect face. The more he permitted surgeons to re-carve his façade, the less handsome he looked. His journey had a grievous destination: he became deformed.

Michael missed the truth that all too many women and girls miss: They are the manifestation of beauty in the first place. Made in the perfect image of our Creator, we are reflections of beauty itself—both in our outward appearance and inward gifts. When Michael died, it saddened me to know he didn't see himself through his Creator's eyes; he was a prisoner behind the mask.

Masks have a way of falling out of place, and when we peek behind them the interior world doesn't always match the façade. Behind his mask, Michael's soul writhed in pain and suffering when all he wanted was to be elevated as a star.

As kids, my best friend and I must have sung along to Whitney Houston's songs a thousand times. We adored her angelic voice, her beauty and talent, her glamour, allure, faith and grace…but what was beneath the hard mask Whitney wore? Abuse, addiction, pain?

When she died, I pondered the illusion of glamour all the more. Pretty outside doesn't mean pretty inside. Because I knew this from my time in the modeling world, my heart empathized with Whitney. I wanted to see her free just as much as her other fans did. Her story is yet another reminder: What we see in pictures is often not akin to reality. Riches don't bring joy and fame doesn't bring fulfillment.

The story of Princess Diana also reveals our preference of image over reality. The world worshipped the façade of romance in her wedding and marriage. But Diana became lonely, bulimic, and terribly unsatisfied with the masquerade. Loving a tragedy, the world capitalized on her drama and the paparazzi hunted her. She died while being chased in a tunnel by a predator so desiring a picture of her pain that he crashed into her car and killed her.

Although the world revered her outward beauty, I believe Diana's true light was her preference for caring for people ravaged by AIDS. Yet her true light was extinguished by the world's obsession with ripping off her porcelain façade in order to reveal how alone she felt.

Honestly, what do we really want? Marilyn to be photographed one last time, Michael to dance for us again, Whitney to sing another solo, Diana to put on the crown and wave her hand? Or do we want to know people as they really are, to care more for their hearts than their fame? If they allow us a glimpse into their insides, unmasking a soul sickness within, will we address their wounds with care and compassion? As fellow human beings, will we offer prayer and space to heal? Or are we really as sick as the paparazzi, seeking to "unmask" the stars as if their suffering were primetime entertainment?

One of the most tragic lies in our world is *you are the mask you wear*. If we are not pinpointing our identity on men, mirrors, or magazines, we focus on the image we project, unworried and unhurried, to make sure it matches our interior truth. The world is famously enthralled by masks, applauding and even worshipping the beautiful people of the world regardless of the possibly ill states of their interior worlds.

This new generation of stars is no exception. Most young, wealthy stars fall. Most rebel against the pressure to be perfect. Most kick and scream by way of drinking or drugs or pushing the boundaries of sexuality. Most don't persist as Disney princesses; most play the rebel or the harlot, at least for a while. Behavior and choices in our world don't define beauty; image does. So the world keeps analyzing their gowns, their shoes, their purses, and their boyfriends, regardless of whether their lives are to be emulated.

The truth is, the stars want just what we want: love, acceptance, worth, purpose, an identity that lasts. But the media just wants a pretty picture for their magazine, a troubled girl with a cover story, or even worse, a picture of a fallen star dragging herself to court for yet another offense. The media wants an image; the girl wants happiness and freedom. It's a tough battle they fight, and most of the time, the girl doesn't win.

Meanwhile the average teenage girl might gaze at the images of the stars, feeling less than beautiful herself. She might think their images look perfect. Then she might run to the mirror and analyze her own image: flawed. Disappointment might reign. Or, she may subconsciously decide choices and attitudes don't define her; life is all about how she looks. So she might get this outfit, or that makeup, or do this workout in hopes she'll measure up—which doesn't satisfy.

The Bible teaches that when we worship images of man instead of our Creator, our hearts become filled with darkness (Romans 1:21-22). Masquerades don't only trap the mask-wearer; the one who fixes her gaze on the mask gets sucked into its lies.

Why are so many girls cutting themselves? Why are so many turning on their bodies? Images of the media have turned their gaze away from their Creator to what is seen. The exalted gods of the stars are held above their heads like lights in the sky. We are to esteem their light, even if there is a rotting mess beneath the brilliant exterior.

Deep down, every girl wants to shine. Every girl wants to be free and beautiful in light of her imperfections. And every girl wants someone to see beyond her exterior shell, peer into her heart, and accept her truth, whatever it may be.

Unmasked

The first high school girls' event I spoke at was called "Unmasked." I was asked to speak at this event during my season of "unmasking," battling cystic acne by fasting from the mirror.

When I arrived at the event, the girls were wearing matching bright blue shirts. They streamed into the building hugging their pillows and toting their overnight bags, huge smiles of anticipation on their faces. A former model was coming to speak to them! Or maybe they were just excited to get out of the house for a huge sleepover, which is the best part. If you knew me you would know I *love* sleepovers!

On Friday night, behind the podium, I followed a very detailed outline of my story. I wasn't a skilled speaker, but I presented my heart on a platter and gave the girls everything I had. That night they went back to the host homes and poured out their own stories with each other. Simply telling my truth inspired them to tell theirs too.

The next morning, something supernatural happened. As I spoke of my struggles with image and value, their battles bobbed to the surface: eating disorders, the pain of their parents' divorces, their mothers' obsession with appearance, rejection at school. I could go on. At times they laughed; at times they cried hot tears and came to support each other at the altar, where they had the opportunity to trade in the lies they'd believed for truth.

I fell in love with the girls—the skinny blondies, the tough athletes, the overweight beauties. I loved the misfits, the cheerleaders, the scholars, the dreamers. But my heart especially wrapped around the lonely and broken ones who didn't feel loved or precious or beautiful—the ones who had believed they were less and needed someone to believe they were made for more.

Unmasking our pain is the beginning of healing. Then there is a point when we stop looking at our pasts and ourselves and choose to look outward. Choosing to help others from the center of our own pain completes our healing and brings our experience full circle. There is nothing more satisfying than taking our past and turning it into a better future for the girl coming up the road behind us.

These days I am blessed to have the opportunity to speak in schools. Before I arrive, I try to talk to the counselor. If anyone knows what goes on behind the masks of junior high and high school girls, she does. Sometimes my heart hurts when I get off the phone with the counselor. I find out things that break my heart. Girls are skipping lunch to be skinnier. Girls are getting weird about food. Girls are dressing promiscuously, yet it's tough to do much about it since they are following their mothers' example. Girls are sharing their bodies with boys, girls are posting sexy images of themselves, girls are harassing each other and cyberbullying. Girls are sometimes overtly jealous and even hateful. Girls are being abused at home. Their parents are critical of their weight or grades. Girls are trying to be the perfect athlete to please Mom and Dad. Girls are cracking under the pressure to perform. Girls—even in junior high—are cutting and forming suicide pacts, or trying to recover from the pain of a friend who hung herself in her bedroom.

And you've called me? I think. Who am I? I am nothing but a girl who raised her hand one day, and said, "Here I am. Send me!" (Isaiah 6:8).

Even with all these issues, the girls are wonderful. Many are making great choices; many are going great places. Lots are hard workers and have a destiny in mind. Some even understand that perfection isn't the goal and realize success is an inside job. Lots of girls want to make huge differences in the world, and they will.

Like women, most girls love honesty and are drawn to authenticity. They love to laugh. Some are loud and crazy; others, introspective.

The vast majority feel good about banding together and supporting each other, even if it's only in their clique. They are devoted to their best friends and stick by each other's sides. A lot of them help each other tell the truth and get help when needed; they believe in each other and speak uplifting words, inspiring each other to believe the best of themselves. Many are highly talented and are good stewards of their gifts. They are filled with faith and hope and real beauty.

This generation of girls is fantastic, and as a voice in their lives, I am incredibly proud of the women they will become. These girls have all the opportunity in the world to be great, yet I know the world will try to rob their innocence, warp their sexuality, burden their hearts, and steal their destiny.

What can I do about suicide pacts and cutting and abuse? What can I do about girls who hate their bodies and hate their fathers and hate themselves?

All I can do is look to God and ask for help. Then I step on the stage and pour out my heart like I did the very first time. The thirsty ones will drink, hopefully.

Sometimes I even shock the girls a little by taking out one of my childhood masks and smashing it with a great big hammer on the stage. The porcelain shards crack, break, and scatter. The hammer's strike and broken pieces thrill them.

When they settle down, a wave of relief washes over their faces. They learn that masquerades hide their real beauty instead of revealing it—something the world has maybe not mentioned yet. I do my best to unmask the lies they have believed and tell them the truth: They are made for more than eating disorders, cutting, and suicide pacts. They are worth more than jealousy, bullying, and sexting. They possess beauty, worth, and purpose. It's up to them to choose: Live like you are less or live like you are more.

Afterward, the girls pour forward. Their stories have gotten knocked loose and surfaced. Like a river whose dam breaks, after the program they are either too broken up to speak or so broken their truths spill. It's such a release for them, and we leave *knowing* we made some impact in the world.

Other times they have to rush off to class before the tardy bell rings, and I find myself longing for more time with them. I want to know they heard me. I want to prevent them from making the same mistakes. I want to save each last one of them.

But I can't. It's time to go, and saving them isn't up to me anyway. It never was.

Beautiful Truth

Sometimes girls hide behind hard masks for fear of getting hurt again. Sometimes their parents force masks on them—and underneath they are stewing because they are taught to live a lie. Other times a mask is a way for a girl to look beautiful on the outside when she doesn't know who she is inside. Deeper still, masks hide our secrets, keeping them buried so our ugliness doesn't surface.

It's dark behind a mask, and hard to see.

Women know this because we wear masks too. We hide our truths in search of acceptance. We avoid "getting real" for fear of what ugliness might come out. We want to look good and we have to protect ourselves from more hurt.

But if we know anything about masks, we know that taking them off and setting them down is the beginning of our truth, and truth sets us free.

I've seen the power of what happens when women get real and get well. When it happens, they can be models for a better life for the next generation.

One of my all-time favorite girls' events was in Cape Cod. I packed my best "Caroline Kennedy" clothes, foolishly assuming the attendees would look like the Kennedys. But when I arrived, the little bayside hotel was filled with girls from the "other side of town." The audience was made up of African-American and Latina girls. Lots of them wore baggy sweatshirts, jeans, tennis shoes, sexy or gang-like attire, and many were overweight.

It seemed like it would be a tough audience for a skinny blonde lady like me, dressed in a black and white striped top, pink button-down sweater, and long skirt and riding boots, appropriately dressed for a lawn party.

But this is my favorite type of audience in all the world, because on the surface you would think they would never relate to me. I opened the event with my usual "medical lesson" about how biologically we are practically identical, and a lot more alike than we are different.

During the event, we had mirrors up at the front of the stage for the girls to write their "lies" on. Throughout the weekend, the lies piled up in multicolored ink written haphazardly all over the mirrors.

When they left the room, Caris, my traveling companion and dear friend, and I read their heartache written out. *I will never be beautiful. I am ugly. No one loves me, not even my father. I am fat and nasty. I will never heal from my rape. Everybody hates me. I am not lovable, not even by God. I am worthless.*

As I said, I love a sleepover, and this event was two nights. The girls had a great opportunity to think about their lies and replace them with truth: They *are* loved, they *are* beautiful, they *are* worth it.

At the end of the event, I put on my crown and some protective goggles, took a mallet, and started smashing the lies on the mirrors. You should have heard those girls whoop and roar as I stood up there in my fancy outfit, smiling like a crazy lady in my goggles and princess crown, shattering their lies, dancing on the broken mirrors with my tall black boots.

In joy, they mobbed the stage. They couldn't wait to grab a hammer and have a crack at their own lie. As the music played, they boogied on the mirrors, grinding the heels of their shoes into the cracks. Cheering and laughing and singing, they stomped on the glass until the words "worthless" and "fat" were crushed and unreadable.

It was Truth they streamed to—Beautiful Truth. Like a lighthouse circling on the bay, Truth beckoned them to travel through the muddy and torrid water of their hearts and climb onto the steady shore of Christ. They saw how they looked in his eyes: adored, forgiven, cherished, made for more.

Multicolored crushed glass adorned the altar. It looked like the pathway of the redeemed, the floor of heaven, precious stones reflecting rainbow light.

Every Disney princess had an evil enemy who was after her heart. She was set to inherit the throne; she rightly possessed the crown as an inheritance from the king. But someone always wanted to steal it from her—whether it was Maleficent, the Mistress of All Evil, devising a plan to injure and silence Sleeping Beauty; the evil stepsisters locking Cinderella in her room; the jealous mother imprisoning Rapunzel; or the evil Sea Witch determined to rob Ariel of her exquisite voice. There is always an enemy lurking to destroy the princess and devour her light.

The evil one is always dark and his eyes are filled with fury. He wants to keep the girl trapped in darkness where he is. He wants to mute her so she cannot bless the world with her beauty. He wants to cover her with a mask and steal her voice, telling her she is not beautiful; not worthy; not loved; and certainly not powerful.

I am all too familiar with this enemy and his lies. At one time he had me muted, sleeping in a depression from which I could hardly be roused. At one time, I hated my reflection in the mirror and felt nothing but ugly and discarded. I considered suicide. I injured myself. I allowed others to abuse me and speak for me. There were heavy chains around my soul but my perfect mask was set in place.

And then a King roused me from my slumber and told me I was made for more. He unlocked my chains, unleashed my lies, and released truth to pour into my heart like sunlight.

When I left the modeling industry, I ran far and fast. Although it offered travel, money, and prestige, I had come to loathe the masquerade. I had seen too many hurting girls behind the pristine facades; too many lost, wandering souls trapped behind demands of perfection; and I too had become a prisoner to the shell. If I was hurting, it wasn't allowed to show; I just had to buck up and be pretty. If I felt degraded or disregarded or disgusted, I had to smile and make nice. I had to stuff my emotions to the point that I became sick. Everything about it went against the grain of my soul's fabric.

Over the years I have found that women and girls across the board hate masks. We are repelled by them yet often trapped behind them. We are afraid to speak the truth and say what hurts; we fear rejection, blame, and shame. Yet we must push through our fears and seek the help we need. Teen suicides, the breakup of marriages that "looked so perfect," and the dissolution of families can be the catastrophic result should we choose the mask over the real. We simply cannot buy into the media's images of perfect beauty that make drama look glamorous, rebellion look appealing, and cover-ups the norm.

Women and girls who do not speak openly of their pain are hard to heal. For me personally, it took years to tell the truth of my experience. But when I did, the journey of healing began. Likewise, the bleeding woman bled for twelve long years before she told Jesus "the whole truth," and in turn he freed her from her prison.

Jesus was always more interested in people who took off the mask than people who made themselves look good. He called mask-wearers white-washed tombs, who looked beautiful on the outside but on the inside were full of the stench of death.

When we do not speak of our pain, it becomes death to us. We turn inward, harming ourselves. When girls feel like they do not have a voice, they can sometimes desire to hurt themselves as a way to release the emotional agony.

When we hurt, God knows the source of our pain and can touch the place only he knows. He'd rather we crack a perfume bottle and pour out every ounce of our souls than stand around looking good to everybody else, pretending we don't need healing.

When we take off our masks, there is nothing separating us from him. We are bare-faced and can face our one true mirror. There, with our masks shattered in a thousand pieces on the ground, we are loved and accepted and changed for the better.

You are more than the mask you wear, and when you are honest about what lies beneath the surface, freedom, healing, and purpose wash the shore of your soul. God's territory is light; God's language is truth. When you walk in the light, you leave the earth imprinted with your realness and beautified by your honesty, and others are inspired to follow your steps. Because we walk in the light, so others want this unmasking.

There is a story in Luke 7:36-50 of one such woman. She was so real it made others uncomfortable, but Jesus loved her.

The Sinful Woman Speaks

My heart is broken. My mind is broken. My body was broken long ago. I don't know how it all began and at this point I see no end. I am caught in a web and cannot get out. I am my sin. I am dirty. Rotten. Used. Fallen. Embarrassed. Ashamed. Without a name. It's like I have no face. No one looks me in the eye anymore; men just use me, but I carry their sin everywhere I go. I carry it in the streets. I carry it in my gait. I carry it in my mind, and my heart is weighed down and tarnished over, mucky stones, nothing but dirt.

Honestly, what do I have to lose if the Messiah rejects me? I'm already rejected. But I feel like when I see him, I'll enter the inner room. And there, I'll just tell the truth. I'm so sorry for how I haven't honored the Lord. I'm so terribly sorry.

But it's not my destiny to keep living this way. I refuse it! I'm running for the light and even though he's at the Pharisee's house tonight, I feel like he's running toward me too.

When I get there, it is just as I supposed: I cry in heaps. I break down right in front of all those proper people. On my knees, I pour out my oil on his feet and wash them with my tears. My gown is soiled and stained, dragging on the floor, and my hair is a mop for the oil. I give him everything I've got.

The Pharisee judges me; he believes wearing a mask when God has come for dinner looks better than messy me. But Jesus—he stands up for me and says, she has loved much, and she is forgiven much. I do love much. I've hurt myself and I've hurt others, but I really love him much.

I hear his voice. "Your sins are forgiven." I look up, and he's my new mirror. His eyes brim with grace. "Your faith has saved you. Go in peace," he says, and I see a new me in his reflection.

With all the guck in my heart poured into the light, he spoke to me. And he changed me for the better. I won't ever walk in my old ways; I'll walk a little closer to the footsteps of my Lord. He is the light of my life, beautiful to me.

You are more than the mask you wear, and when you take off the mask and be honest about what lays beneath the surface, freedom, healing, and purpose wash the shore of your soul. In turn, you leave the earth imprinted with your realness, beautified by your honesty, and others are inspired to follow your steps. Because you walk in the light, so we want this unmasking, where all is healed, all is made well.

You Are a Shining Light

Lanterns made up of broken pieces cast the prettiest light.

The Most Beautiful Woman in the World

Last year, *People* revealed its "Most Beautiful Woman in the World," her goddess-like image selling the cover while we saw her skin, hair, clothes, and body plastered on television, in music videos, reality TV, commercials, you name it.

At home after a long day, relaxing on the couch with our families (or more realistically, still doing dishes and getting the kids to bed), us moms might feel slightly "less than" as all jaws drop at the stars' incredible good looks. As women we are not human if we feel no effect from these images. Maybe we are tired or worn out from long days. Maybe our skin has broken out or we are battling weight issues. Maybe we are dealing with the impending death of a loved one or a financial crisis. How can we ever compete with that beauty on television?

Yet the very month *People* named her the "Most Beautiful Woman in the World," the woman's marriage fell to pieces—and I say this not with judgment but with sincerity. Divorce is horribly painful. It is the shattering not only of promises but of dreams and futures. Ignoring this truth, however, the world applauded the Most Beautiful Woman in the World with lots of follow-up articles and TV shows revealing how fantastic she looked while going through her divorce.

The media subtly let us know, "You too can break up your marriage and look fab doing it!" Or even worse, "Why do you look so bad? What's the big deal if your family falls apart? Just start dating someone else! You too can get divorced and be radiant!"

Divorce tears a woman's heart, sometimes to shreds. The breakup of a family is excruciating, and it's a lie to think that anyone can look fabulous while enduring it. It's a façade.

Maybe I'm too sympathetic or transparent, but masks like that scare me. I know what it's like to live for the façade of beauty and go home suffering. I know what it's like to long for love and acceptance while everyone is applauding you. It's painful, and it's real.

In no way am I surprised when I open a tabloid and see the page entitled "Divorce of the Week." There we see yet another hurting "star." Last time I looked, that same "star" was on a later page, listed as one of those "ageless beauties" we should imitate.

What is worth imitating? Creaseless faces or happy marriages? What is beautiful? A great body, a glittering gown, or lasting love and a happy family?

The "curse of the Oscar" is infamous in Hollywood; from the years 2001 to 2010, six winners for Best Actress experienced the heartbreak of their marriages shattering at the time they won the Oscar. As they unveiled their exquisite gowns and rich adornments, dripped in costly fabric and pricy jewels, and accepted their trophies to grand applause, the primary relationship in their life shattered, and their children were left with the fallout.

In this case, I'm not looking at the way stars are different from us. I am looking at the way they are the same. As gorgeous as they may be on the outside, we are similar within. Just like us, they long to find contentment and beauty in their homes.

For now we are left with this question: What is beautiful? What is worth applauding? What is stellar and amazing and victorious for women? Is it really about the accomplishment, the trophy, the applause? Or is it something no one sees? Is allure more about the way we treat our husbands at the end of the day, beauty really about the way we talk to our kids in the morning, and radiance all about where we look for our guidance?

Or are we really only as pretty as the masks we wear?

The Morning Star Speaks

Masks are shells, a protective covering for a tender core, the outer armor guarding the roar of the spirit. Masks are not always bad. Sometimes people have to put on the face and fake it 'til they make it; it's a mode of combat in a coarse world. My daughters get thick-skinned from battle; it's natural and can even be good.

What's not good is falsehood. Pretending leads to sorrow. Lies get buried beneath the surface, pain gets masked, and no one heals. Transparency is beautiful; people are attracted by it. I never had to be fake because I knew who I was and whose I was. My identity was my truth; this freed me to share my truth without reservation.

There used to be a curtain in the temple that separated people from entering my presence. Now there is none. It tore when I died on the cross. You can pass through the curtain now. You can come to God with an unmasked face, bearing your truth.

I love your truth, yet I know your lies.

For just a moment on the mountain, I showed my friends my whole truth—all that I am on the inside. Shedding the cloak of my humanity, I allowed my glory to turn inside out. Of course it was so dazzling, bright white like the sun, that they fell over speechless and shut their eyes. My honesty was almost too much for them.

People were drawn to me because of the flickering flame I was within—it certainly wasn't my good looks or great talent! I never sought fame. I came to serve. People experienced the lamb and the lion within me. That's what they fell in love with—my heart.

Lucifer, on the other hand, loved the outside of things. He took great pride in his good looks and he wanted to be worshipped for his wealth, wisdom, and beauty. He aspired to be a star above all stars, even calling himself the son of the dawn. But no matter how good he looked on the outside, his desire to be exalted above my Father made him the ugliest beast.

People worship the movie stars and don't know why it doesn't make them feel good about themselves. Especially the young ones. The more they look at images of the stars, the worse they feel. When you worship images made to look like man, your hearts are dimly lit. When you worship me, I pour my radiance into your heart.

And the beauty and value I give lasts.

The Light of the World

All fall short of the glory of God. None of us can go up to a mountain like Jesus did and turn ourselves inside out, blazing white. Men have their time of glory. They rise but then fall. Everyone's fate is the same: We turn to dust and our spirits return to God.

In America we worship outward beauty, talent, and the appearance of greatness. Yet time and time again we discover that behind the mask of success is fallen humanity.

But some stars basking in the limelight of the world's most celebrated stages are also shining brilliant lights in kids' hospital rooms. Behind the scenes, some stars are walking the war-torn areas of the world, carrying water. Some are carrying babies right out of the darkest, most hopeless settings and giving them homes where love reigns. Some of their marriages are surviving and thriving.

Everyone is inspired when athletes and musicians and actresses impact the world with uncomplicated love. We appreciate it when they understand that to whom much is given, much is expected.

Deep down we all realize that real stars wash dirty feet and touch lepers and let the children come to them.

We know their life behind the mask is the most important life they live.

Herein rests my greatest concern: the girls of this generation will believe shining their light abroad is more important than shining their light at home. There's no "Lights, camera, action!" at home— no makeup and no trophies for a job well done.

I know this all too well. At one time in my experience, I started believing that being a light to the world meant the world outside these walls where my family lives. Now I am convinced that being a light to the world begins here at home.

The Covering

I am standing in the empty airport, shivering in the sweater wrapped around me like a too-thin blanket. It's three in the morning, and I have missed my connection and ended up in the wrong city. I am walking along, praying for an angel to come and help me.

Then I see this woman in an American Airlines uniform, a big rack of keys hanging on her belt loop. I tell her my issue—I've lost my bag and I have no way to get home from this place.

She lets me into the baggage room and my bag is not there. I call my husband, and he tries to tell me what to do to get home. But I disagree with him and begin to argue.

The woman taps me on the shoulder. "Excuse me," she says respectfully, her blue eyes gentle yet firm. "I need to tell you something. Can you tell him to hold on just a moment?"

I excuse myself from Shane and press the receiver to my chest so he can't hear me.

"Are you a believer?" she asks.

"Yes," I say.

"I thought so. God wants me to tell you something."

"Yes?"

"You need to listen to your husband. He is your spiritual covering," she says, making a motion like she is outlining an umbrella above her head. "God will speak through him. I can explain this more later, but for now, just do whatever he tells you. Do *not* argue with him."

"Okay…" I say, somewhat in disbelief.

I get back on the phone. "I'm sorry, honey, what were you saying I should do?"

That certainly settled the matter.

When I got off the phone, she told me that if I ever go out of my husband's covering, it's like jutting out into the rain instead of staying under the safety of the umbrella. There will be angst and turmoil, she tells me. Stay in your husband's covering; it will protect you.

I nodded my head like I understood. But it would take tragedy and trials, years later, for me to really understand it.

Broken

When I was writing *Girl Perfect*, I studied all the verses that refer to beauty. I was shocked and even a bit scared to discover that pride in external beauty began with Satan. It made me realize how much he had me duped when I was modeling. At the same time, it made a lot of sense. As the "prince of this world," he has a host of women and girls worshipping outward beauty as well. I went on to write the *Girl Perfect Study Guide* to offer healing truths to women and girls. The study also clearly reveals the lies of Satan, who is the author of the masquerade, death, and all things ugly.

Through our events and resources like these, our message became like a city on a hill, drawing people to its authenticity, inspiring them to reject masks and pursue God.

I'm not sure if it happened in a day, a week, a month, or a year, but the next thing you knew it felt like someone was trying to rip my life to shreds.

An internationally acclaimed organization that provides support for third-world children contacted me to see if I would become their representative. They also asked if I could join them on a trip to an impoverished area in South America in just a few short months. I was pregnant with Samuel, so we checked with our doctor and he seemed fine with the trip.

But my husband was hesitant about it, saying he detected pride in my voice when I talked about the opportunity. Foolishly, I dismissed his concern. We sought advice, received encouragement to go, and decided to take the trip.

A few days before the plane was to take off, we went to get immunized. The nurse told us she could not vaccinate me because of my pregnancy. She also said she would not in good conscience advise me to go to this area of the world while pregnant; the risk of contracting diseases was too high and if that happened, I could harm or lose the baby.

With less than 48 hours before our plane took off, I called the organization. They assured me we would not be in diseased territory and all the food and water would be safe. But Shane felt the trip wasn't worth risking me or the baby. Forgetting what the woman in the airport had told me, I felt such a strong obligation to the organization that I argued with him. I called my doctor for another opinion. When he learned the details of the situation, he recommended I not go.

I called my mentor, Devi, who travels all around the world to impoverished nations. She told me that if my husband and doctor didn't agree with it, the answer was no...and that was it.

I had a very strong independent streak rooted in traveling around the world by myself as a young woman, depending on no one but myself. (My rebellious streak was so strong as a teen that I had a bumper sticker on my car that read "Question Authority!") Unlike those of you who grew up in the church, the words *submission, honor,* and *headship* were foreign to me.

My husband, on the other hand, grew up in the South, where women generally honored their husband's voices and men built protective hedges around their families. So, fiercely protective of his wife and cubs, my husband went up against fiercely independent me, who wanted to save the hungry children of the world.

After debating the risks with my husband, the doctors, and the organization which insisted everything would be safe, I was frustrated and exhausted. They had two plane tickets for us and I felt a strong commitment and obligation to them.

We are at the point in this story where my commitments and obligations were falling on the wrong side of the fence. My husband's voice should have been first.

So who did I listen to?

Them or him?

I should go to South America and look at the suffering! I thought. *I should believe a faithful God will protect me! It is my purpose to shine a light for the hungry!* I wanted to offer a child a cup of water that would sustain him for his entire life—and then come back to the States and find more people to support more children! What a blessing! I wanted to do such a good thing.

This was not the only area of our lives where I was questioning and arguing with him. You name the topic, I was balking at his leadership. If he had deep feelings and concerns that begged to be authenticated, I dismissed them as unreasonable and invalid.

In public I was teaching girls to honor God by honoring their bodies, but in private I wasn't listening to my own head. The Bible teaches that man is the head and woman is the body, and a house divided will not stand.

In the midst of my arguing with Shane about the safety of the trip, we received news that a car bomb went off in the city where we were traveling. I became so weak with morning sickness I couldn't even lift myself off the couch.

Then, tragedy struck. Due to the distractions of this incessant division, I failed to care for our sweet dog, Dallas, who was suffering. Like an alarm blaring in the night, her sudden death put our family in a state of shock and woke me from my stupor. Why was I elevating children across the world over the ones in my home? Why was the voice of any organization more highly esteemed than the voice of my husband? What had happened to me? How could I be so stubborn and foolish?

Our children's hearts were broken, Shane was devastated, and I felt like someone had taken a baseball bat and knocked me to my knees.

We buried Dallas late that night, putting notes in her grave, the whole family weeping and wailing. "Forgive me," were the only words I could pen. The pain was so raw and my sin so apparent, I crawled, pregnant, sobbing to her grave, while Shane's father comforted me.

It was before dawn when I fell to my face in a mess of tears. The pages of my Bible, falling apart at the seams, lay before me. Begging God to speak to me, I parted the Word and found that a chunk from the book of Isaiah had fallen out. The words leaped out at me:

> Although the Lord gives you the bread of adversity and the water of affliction, your teachers will be hidden no more; with your own eyes you will see them. Whether you turn to the right or to the left, your ears will hear a voice behind you, saying, "This is the way; walk in it" (Isaiah 30:20-21).

"More," I whispered. "Show me more."

On the backside of the loose pages: "Put your house in order" (Isaiah 38:1).

That morning Shane woke with eyes red from tears.

"You don't listen to me!" he said.

"I'm sorry! I'm sorry," I cried.

"How can I be your husband if you don't listen to me?"

The woman in the airport told me my husband was my covering, that I wasn't to argue with him, that God would speak through him, that going outside of his covering would cause nothing but turmoil and angst.

Every day, all I felt was turmoil and angst. Every day.

As one hurries toward a warm fire to escape the blistering cold, I went to Devi's house that night. Collapsing in tears on her couch, I huddled by her still and steady light past midnight. Wise women are never afraid to speak the truth, and Devi spoke so gently yet directly it further broke my heart.

"Something insidious happens to us," Devi explained. "We start out on the 'servant' track, and without even realizing it, we've switched tracks and are on the 'self' track."

The truth about my pride and rebellion came into the light. In the light, we see how our sin hurts others and hurts ourselves. Nothing is hidden.

Offering me a picture of marriage, Devi directed my attention to the coffee table—the husband as the table top and the wife as the legs upholding him.

Never before could I see so clearly how I needed to change.

Even though my family forgave me in compassion and mercy, I hung my head in my home for a long time. I constantly felt like I was failing my husband and children. Things in our life were beginning to go terribly wrong, with complicated issues with our extended families, damaged relationships, betrayal and lies, and worries, fears, and insecurities over situations beyond our control. It felt like we were being torn apart from all sides.

I spent a long time looking down at the mess. Always focused on the mess—the circumstance, the past, the regret, the foolishness, the choices I made and others made. I was always staring at the ashes.

I'll say it again: the more you look at something, the more you reflect it. So naturally, my face began to reflect sorrow.

Joy removed itself from me, and this had a grave impact on my closest relationships.

Finally, we sold our house and car and moved into a new neighborhood to try to start fresh.

That's when the mirror shattered into a million little pieces in the big old house we left behind. When we left that house, we left the beautiful lie that you are as pretty as the mask you wear. We left behind the lie that says shining a light outside the home is more important than shining a light within it. We left behind the battle of the wills, and over time, Shane and I came into alignment. We learned that the man is the head of the home, and yet he leads with a quiet strength most effective when met with honor and respect from his wife. This honor trickles down to the children. The greatest way I can trust God is by trusting my covering.

Shane makes a very handsome umbrella from the storm and the rain. It's warm there, in his embrace.

Coming under my husband's umbrella means holding him high. Putting him first. Trusting his protection and yielding to it. Because I had to be my own umbrella for so long, I wrestled with the handle in my marriage. I believed I was wiser, I was stronger, I was higher. This exalted view of myself led to a long season of humbling.

God always brings beauty from the ashes.

Radiant

In our new town, I became surrounded by radiant women. Every time I turned around, I met another woman who had conquered obstacles as painful as can be imagined. Women who had lost their children, their husbands, and their best friends. Women whose marriages were hanging by a thread at one time, but who had stories of how God ventured in and stitched their families back together. One thing they had in common: they learned how to navigate storms by keeping their gaze fixed not on the circumstance but on the Son at the horizon.

Shane's mother, Linda, is one of those radiant women. Psalm 34:5 says, "Those who look to him are radiant; their faces are never covered with shame." Although she has had reason to hang her head many a day, she looks to Jesus as her light. In return, she reflects it.

Linda has told me many times that my joy is mine, and no one can take it from me. She has been through tremendous trials. The rebellion of both of her children when they were teenagers brought her on a long and painful journey. She lived in a large home in those days, and she describes how a shaft of light used to come through the front window in the entry. She used to lie in the shaft of light in the fetal position, the emotional pain too excruciating. Finally she surrendered her children, giving to God what she could not control. In return, she received peace.

And for Linda, for all the storms she has been through, there have been many rainbows.

During my season of trial, I would go to Linda's house just to sit on her couch so I could be near her. She is like a warm fire on a storm-tossed day.

When I felt like my life was in tatters, she had faith God would stitch it back together. When you hit the storm, she said, God will make a rainbow. She lifted my chin up.

Women who shine are women who know: We are a light at home; we are a light abroad. We are not one without the other.

Before we are a true light to the world outside our home, we are a light within it. We are never one without the other.

The Morning Star Speaks

When you trip and fall, your perfect mask falls off and breaks into shattered shards. It may hurt you, but I can put them back together in a more beautiful pattern, through which I can shine a more luminous light.

In the old days, potters would toss out their broken pottery and the lantern makers would go out to the field to collect the shards. They would use the pieces for their lanterns because light shone beautifully through the cracks.

You ask me to make you more like me, and then one day you feel shattered. I know what that feels like, and it doesn't change your identity. You are still my daughter, my creation, my temple gate called Beautiful. When you allow me to shine through the broken pieces of your heart, people will be drawn to your lamp, because it will be a softer light on their darkened day.

The very first clue that pointed to the Messiah was a star in the sky. Then, when he grew up, Jesus proclaimed, "I am the light of the world" (John 8:12).

He knew we would get all confused and think who we are is a reflection of where we've been, the mistakes we've made, or the masks we wear. So he let us know: You find out who you are in the reflection of who I am. I am the light of the world; you are the light of the world. He didn't say, you *will be* a light to the world *when you* go here and do this good thing; he didn't say we *become* a light because we do everything right. He simply said, "You are the light" (Matthew 5:14).

Jesus was careful to point out we are both a public light and a private light—and people will be drawn to the light in us. "A town built on a hill cannot be hidden. Neither do people light a lamp and put it under a bowl. Instead they put it on its stand, and it gives light to everyone in the house" (Matthew 5:14-15).

Realizing that I am not only a town built on a hill but a lamp in my home, I always have to look to him for my reflection. The more we look at something, the more we reflect it. Jesus was a man who suffered, who ate the bread of adversity and drank the water of affliction, yet in him there was fullness of joy. He fully submitted; he fully honored.

I don't know why we suffer, but I do know walking through the fire can make us shine all the more when we come out.

Esther Speaks

Women, you can be both a lamp at home and a light abroad. My power came from knowing that my light outside of the home began with my light inside it.

My husband was no perfect man. My husband got drunk and believed a lie. It's hard to respect a drunk man or a fool, but simple to choose to honor the king inside of him.

I saved my people from sheer destruction—yes, I rescued them from death. But it began with what happened when no one was looking.

I cared for my body, I performed beauty treatments, and I looked my best. But you know who it was for? My husband, the king. And even when he acted a fool, I served him. When I needed to address the dire situation my people were in, I did not force it on the man. I waited for the right time. I prepared his food. I prayed.

When you do this, you will have more power because your outward beauty matches your inward humility. Of course he esteemed my request to save my people and slay their murderer, for I first esteemed him.

The Lion and the Lamb

The story of Esther teaches us that the best way to save people and slay the murderer is to exalt the king in our own homes.

I've always told people my life verses were 1 Peter 3:3-4: "Your beauty should not come from outward adornment, such as elaborate hairstyles and the wearing of gold jewelry or fine clothes. Rather, it should be that of your inner self, the unfading beauty of a gentle and quiet spirit, which is of great worth in God's sight."

Over time I have pondered those verses, because I'm not a gentle and quiet personality. I'm more like a lion. I can growl. I can be fierce. Yet Jesus was both the lion and the lamb. He could have come to earth with his fangs posed to devour, eyes blazing, prepared to unleash his wrath on fallen man. But instead he chose to come in gentle grace. He moved through the earth as one who forgave, one who washed feet instead of pointing out the grime, one who touched those tortured by demons rather than avoiding their anguish.

The verses on either side of 1 Peter 3:3-5 are the key to our light. They say we win our husbands not with our words, but with our behavior. This was how the holy women of the past used to adorn themselves—with honor.

My husband loves it when I read to him. I do most of my writing while reading aloud. There is something about my reading voice that puts Shane at rest. One time I was reading to him and he became mesmerized. "You should speak like that all the time," he said. "I would do whatever you say."

Like God, men are not moved by our demands. Men are moved by our faith. The gentle and quiet spirit that is so powerful is the Holy Spirit. We are the vessels of God. He is our light, and we are broken lanterns through which he shines.

The Spirit of the Lord is gentle, kind, controlled. It is filled with the elements of true beauty: faith, hope, and love. Jesus teaches us what love is: laying down our lives. Lifting others high.

What if woman's beauty is not about exalting herself, but instead, humbling herself? Surely, it is laying down her lion with her lamb.

9

The Fifth Lie:

You Are Mastered by the Media

Be careful, little eyes, what you see.

The Master Speaks

The media is a vehicle, as a car is a vehicle. A vehicle can be safe and get you where you want to go.

But a vehicle can also be used to seek, kill, and destroy. Accidents can happen. Kids can drive too fast, not realizing the effect of their actions. Mothers can get distracted by the children in the backseat and not see the road in front of them. People can get drunk or high or too tired and drive into a ditch and die. It happens.

The media is like a vehicle.

Drive carefully.

Use with caution.

The slightest turn can run you off the road.

Fix your eyes straight ahead. Do not turn to the right or the left. Keep your eye on the goal and remember: You are the master of the vehicle. You control it. It doesn't control you.

If you ever feel like it's controlling you, take your foot off the gas, pull to the side, put it in park, get out of the car, and call for help. I'll help you put some guards in place to make sure you know. You are the master; don't let it master you.

The screens are everywhere. Before we talk about how bad they can be, we've got to say how great they are. I love being able to text simple notes to our daughter on her phone or send out a funny video of Samuel. Throughout the writing of this book, my friends have encouraged and challenged me to press on, via text. I love a great movie, am crazy about my Bible software program, and seriously appreciate the Internet. It makes it possible to reach people across the planet and put our thumbprints on the world.

Yet we cannot deny the dangers of the screens—the way they separate us from people and distract us from living fully in the moment, because on our screen our minds are in another place. It is like a vehicle, driving us to great destinations or terrible ones. Unfortunately, what comes through the screen can have a tremendously negative impact on us.

For boys, it starts with video games. They play them for hours and hours and hours. It becomes what they love. Then, as they get older, a click of a button instantly funnels them into a world they have hopefully never seen. This world, like the games, is endless. It is a plethora of pornographic images that ignite arousal and incite addiction. It leaves them feeling shamed, but now they know it's there. All it takes is a click of the button.

It used to be the closest a boy could get to looking up a woman's skirt was running under the mannequins in the mall to take a peek. As he got older he might have rummaged through a National Geographic magazine or the underwear section in the JC Penney catalogue. When he grew up, he may have even ventured to the liquor store to peek at an X-rated magazine. But would he subscribe to it? Where would he have it sent? His house? His college dorm? Doubtful. And when he got married, how could he hide that subscription from his wife and kids? He couldn't.

Looking at pornography used to take thoughtful, premeditated effort. Now it takes about this long: click, click, click, you're there. Mom's footsteps up the stairs, one click, gone.

After a hundred clicks, his future wife won't be amazing anymore. After a thousand, he could be totally wrecked for her, tormented by the constant awareness of what is behind that screen—which isn't just in his room, but in his back pocket. The torture of what looks so desirable on the surface and the power it has to control him if he lets it can derail him completely. He hasn't even met the tender wife of his youth yet or tasted her sweetness, and she's already sour.

Picture Time!

For the girls, media images are ever so complicated. First off, they have the even mildly pornographic images to contend with— images they can't live up to, images which aren't even real. Even if the girl knows her value is more than her flesh, the images present women as pawns to be used and displayed and sexualized, instead of sacred creatures made in the image of God. These images have the potential to act as distorting prisms, skewing a girl's image of herself, sex, and her husband.

This generation of girls has to deal with a generation of boys whose heads are filled with these images. It's a different world for girls than it was for us, and it's hard on them even before they've kissed a boy—and even harder afterward.

Every little girl wants to be a star, for everyone to gaze at her image and *ooh* and *aah*. Social media sites give her that opportunity. She can post pictures of herself and everyone can say, "Thumbs up!" "Wow!" "Like!"

For lots of girls in search of approval—and especially for those who have suffered rejection—something twisted happens. They begin to think their likability is related to their online image. They keep switching their profile picture in hopes of getting more likes, and when they get older they try sexy shots and earn approval.

Now they are like a Victoria's Secret model and everyone is ogling their photos. "Aren't you amazing!" "You look so beautiful!" "You go girl!"

Girls like taking pictures and making albums—it's natural for us. I did it when I was a kid, but the albums were just for me and my friends. The pictures stayed in my bedroom.

"My page *is* just for my friends," the girls cry! I'm sorry, but no one has 238 close friends. I have ten, max. And of those ten, I would only have a sleepover with five. And of those five, only two would actually sit with me and look at all the pictures in my album, and they would only do that because they really love me, not because they want to see every single one. The only person who wants to see every single picture of me is my mother.

The vehicle of the media can be very deceptive. On the surface we see what looks like an online photo album or a fun way to share pictures or connect with friends. But beneath that mask, trouble can be brewing. If a girl gets a text or is notified every time someone likes her picture or approves of her post, that's bad. Because every time she gets a text, she is interrupted. Our girls don't need to be constantly interrupted from their studies, their sports, and their families to be told someone liked their picture or agreed with their thought. No wonder they are on a roller coaster ride; no wonder they have image problems. Social media isn't just a way for kids to connect; it's a way for kids to instantly and constantly approve or disapprove of images of one another and of themselves. Cameras used to point outward, capturing memories. Today, they point inward.

Why are the girls constantly changing their profile pictures? To keep up with the new look? Just to be girls and have fun? Or is it because some of them actually believe the lie of the masquerade— that their image as they present it in the media is the image they possess? They are as pretty as their picture. As worthy as their number of likes.

I mentored a girl who had this issue. She was my student in

eighth grade, when I used to teach writing after I left the modeling industry. Rejected by her mother, dealing with her parents' divorce, feeling controlled and manipulated by her dad, she began cutting at age 12. She used to duck into my classroom at lunch because it was a safe harbor for her troubled heart.

Years later, she found me through Facebook. In communicating with her, I noticed her profile pictures were always changing to be more and more seductive. Never afraid to tell her the truth, I sent her a message, advising her to take the photos down, that they dishonored her future husband and children. She soon called me to confess she had a full-fledged eating disorder, was addicted to drugs, promiscuous, stripping, delusional, and suicidal.

Together, she and I pounded on the door of Mercy Ministries, an excellent in-house long-term treatment center for troubled young women, and by a miracle she got in.

When she graduated from Mercy, she called me to tell me how much God had illuminated things for her. Leaving a message on my phone, she said, "Call me back! I'm not well enough yet to have a cell phone—or Internet—or screens of any sort. So you can just reach me on the landline."

You bet I'll reach you on the landline, girlfriend. You bet I will.

When girls post pictures of themselves via text, email, or social media, those pictures become public, and all someone has to do is click on a photo and save it to a hard drive. Then, even if the girl regrets publishing those photos of herself and takes them off the Internet, someone else has them saved.

The Internet is very deceptive. Anyone can pose as anyone. People who think "only my friends can see my page" are fooling themselves. Any jerk can pose as a friend and get a window into your personal life if you post it online. It's not difficult at all. For the girls, any bully can click on a girl's photo and pose as her. Then that bully can say all kinds of horrible things about other people through "her" mouth. It's identity theft, but the Internet makes it easy.

But worse than all that, if women or girls take sexual photos of themselves and share them, someone can decide to turn the little dream into a nightmare. That person can take the racy picture and turn it into a website, and she can do nothing about it. Or even sicker, someone can take a decent photo of a girl and Photoshop it to look like her head is on a nude body. Later in life, her husband and children will have to contend with those photos.

You may think I'm being a little radical here, but you really can't argue with me, because I'm right. I know what I'm talking about and I am warning you: Keep your privates private, keep your kids sacred, and just know you are getting a big thumbs-up from heaven when you guard what is entrusted to you. Guard your body, your marriage, your kids, your future, and the possibility of your great influence in the world.

Do You Like Me Now?

When I was presenting this book to potential publishers, a very reputable one wanted to know how many "likes" I had on Facebook and how many followers I had on Twitter. This was a legitimate marketing question, but I chuckled.

Uh, not enough probably? I thought. I had spent the last eighteen months face-to-face with our new baby. The number of friends I had on Facebook was the last thing on my mind, and at the time I didn't even have a Twitter account.

My marriage and family were center stage. My home life was all I cared about. And when I did engage in public ministry, the greatest impact was in talking to girls in the hallways between sessions, hearing their stories in the book line, and staying after the event to engage with moms and daughters. Yet my greatest ministry happened in my back-yard with my kids, resting my head for longer than planned on their pillows at night, hearing about their days, their battles, their dreams.

The face-to-face is where the real stuff happens, and when we become mastered by the media, hooked to the screen, we can miss it.

Some of the most influential women I know are teachers without Facebook pages—and if they have them, they don't broadcast their every good deed to the world. They teach kids to read and to honor their parents without it being announced with a bullhorn. Others sit face-to-face with troubled teens in counseling offices and hand them a tissue to dry their tears; they are the arms that hug the hurting without having to tell the world about it.

I am surrounded by people who don't need the thumbs-up from the world. My best friend's husband is famous, but she rejects social media so she can focus on her true friends and family. My husband barely touches Facebook and, through his ministry to our sons, is raising two solid boys. When he teaches them to mow the lawn, he doesn't post it to see how many people will approve. I'm the one who wants to share it with everybody! He doesn't care if no one sees.

When I first wrote *Girl Perfect*, I became overwhelmed with administrative tasks. A widow named Jan was looking for a place to serve. She literally came to my house and told me she liked to do "busy work." What a godsend! Over the next five years, Jan wrapped and shipped books and performed a host of other duties, praying we would reach girls. Her service was seen by God, not man, and she never wanted it any other way. And Caris, who founded the ministry with me, doesn't do social media. She goes mountain biking with girls. She takes them out on her boat and stays up late under the stars, hearing their stories and quietly, gently, ushering them toward a walk with God.

Real intimacy, real friendship, real truth, real life happens in the face-to-face, something this generation of girls can miss if they aren't careful. We need to teach them that a friend isn't someone you just met or barely know; it's an intimately connected supporter of your life. And the number of friends you have online or the number of likes you get is no indicator of your value, nor does it measure your influence.

We also need to teach girls that privacy is good. At one time, who we were dating, who we liked, and the things we believed in stayed in our small circle. Now, girls make all of that public. It used to be that when a girl got engaged, it was an intimate moment between her and her future lover. Now it's blasted all over the screen—everyone gets a window in. Same goes for their weddings, their babies, their children growing up.

And for some reason, many are under the impression they need to tell everyone what they are doing and where they are all the time. Telling people our locations is also foolish because it makes us vulnerable. You really want people to know when you're not home? Not a smart idea for your kids.

When does the personal publicity stop? When life gets hard? When dreams crash? When something bad happens? Or is that public too? For many it is. I have a friend who blasted her marital problems all over Facebook, and guess what? She got divorced, and everything she had written to her hundreds of "friends" about the situation became public record. Sad as it is, someday someone could print the whole saga out for her children, and if they read everything she felt, said, and accused her husband of, it would only further devastate three children who are already shattered.

Proverbs 4:23 cautions us, "Above all else, guard your heart, for everything you do flows from it." What are we to guard? Our hearts? Who's got our hearts? Our husbands, our kids, our families.

There is also wisdom in following the example of Jesus's life. He spoke to the multitudes, sharing his teaching with as many as he could and telling them stories. Then he pulled aside his twelve disciples and shared the deeper meaning of the stories with them.

But his most intimate truth he shared only with those in his private circle. When he went up to the mountain he showed Peter, James, and John who he really was. There on the mountain he showed his glory, his robe becoming blazing white, brighter than all the bleach in all the world could make it. He made everything clear—not to the multitudes, but to his most intimate friends. And there, on that mountain, when he was as open and honest and real as he ever was going to get, God spoke to them. They heard his voice.

You know what Jesus told them when they came down from the mountain? Keep this private. Don't tell anyone until I've been raised from the dead (Matthew 17:9).

Jesus believed in keeping some things secret, and he had the wisdom to know when a truth could free someone and when it could make them stumble. He didn't always want attention for every great thing he did. When he performed miracles, he didn't want it broadcast everywhere. In fact, he told people: *Tell no one. Say nothing about this.*

That's right. He would do something great and tell people *not* to post it, *not* to share it.

Jesus's most beautiful interactions with people happened face-to-face, one-on-one. And when he suffered, he didn't look to the multitudes for answers; he looked to the Father.

As far as I can tell, he really lived for an audience of One.

And he has more fans than anyone on the earth.

Who's the Master?

It is the middle of the night. I have been writing a Bible study and my brain has been immersed in the Word for weeks. I've been studying the enemy and the differences between him and Christ. My brain is so wallpapered with what I've been reading that the Word is my only filter right now. I come outside of my office to make some tea and see that *The Bachelor* is on the screen. It's funny, it's crazy, it's completely ridiculous.

As I am waiting for my tea to boil, all of a sudden I see something true in a flash, like a film on fast-forward: *The Bachelor* is the lie of man. It's about worshipping man, believing what he thinks about you. *Extreme Makeover* is the lie of the mirror. It's about the poundage and the measurements declaring your worth. *Project Runway* is the lie of the magazine. It's the worship of outward beauty at the expense of others. *Survivor* awards the best deceiver while *CSI* is all about murder.

Oh no! I think. The enemy is behind all of this. He is working his way into our homes by upholding all of his values through the screen.

But here's the deal. I don't want to be Amish. I love *American Idol*, and I'm not missing *Survivor* next season. Our son plays video games and our daughter watches TV. Shane and I might even cue up some *Bachelor* for a good laugh, and Olivia and I definitely have our eye on *The Biggest Loser.*

But it's not lost on me that "idol" is in the title and "loser" is a dig on overweight people. I'm not naïve enough to think the camera is going to record the pain of the girls who don't win *America's Next Top Model*; I know how many girls lose at the expense of the one who wins, and I know the one who wins may not win in the end. I understand that deceit is the premise of *Survivor*. I get that in the world of the screen god adultery is glamorized, sex before marriage is praised, and in a weird way, murder is glorified.

The screens just aren't as simple as they used to be! It used to be *Leave it to Beaver* and *Happy Days*. Now it's *Modern Family* and *16 and Pregnant.*

What about the video games? Boys used to play Pac Man and Asteroids; now it's a bloodbath.

At some point we cross a line. It's no longer entertainment when the violence and overt sexuality are being replicated in the lives of our kids. Why are we so surprised when boys want to do target practice on real people and girls want to experiment with girls? In video games, boys get points for killing people; they get promoted. On TV, girls get attention for being a teen mom or making out with other girls. There are no repercussions on TV. In video games, there are no grieving mothers or outraged communities to contend with; death is a bonus. There is no human emotion involved. There is no loss of limb that ruins someone's dreams, no bullet that alters a person's working brain, no quadriplegics or kids in physical therapy for the rest of their lives because of that bullet. And there certainly are no bars imprisoning the shooter for life.

We are fools to think the screen god doesn't have anything to do with the death of our children's values. Kids can go online and learn how to build bombs, kill themselves, starve their bodies, explore their sexuality, and more. The culture reflects what the screen instructs them to do. The influence is real and can make us sick, sick, sick.

When our eyes are opened, what do we do? Do we reject media altogether? Do we turn off the screens completely and attempt to live like they don't exist? Up to you. But in my family, the answer is no. I believe we have to see, know, and understand what the world believes. We have to keep our ear to the sound of the world and our ear to the sound of the Word.

At the Cape of Good Hope, at the southern tip of South Africa, the Indian and Atlantic Oceans collide in a majestic yet violent embrace. They crash and explode against the cape. Explorers used to die trying to navigate this collide. Their boats would crash and they would lose sight of the shore. These days it's still a wild trip, but it's possible to round the Cape of Good Hope.

Navigating the collide between the world and the Word is challenging but possible. You just have to keep your eye on the lighthouse, your ear tuned to the captain, and know how to steer clear of the dangers.

For every great battle, there is an enemy. He pursues you, trying to take you and the people in your boat out of the race. Know your enemy. He exalts himself. He exalts fame. He exalts deceit. He exalts the flesh. He exalts death. He exalts sexual sin. He exalts adultery.

He exalts theft. He exalts the outward appearance. He exalts everything but our great and awesome God.

And he works through the screen.

Let's throw a wrench into this discussion. What if God, not
Satan, is the mastermind of the media? What if it was his idea in the
first place to connect people across the globe through a screen? What
if he wanted it first? What if he loves a great tragedy and a fantastic
romance? What if he even has a vested interest in training our sons
for combat? What if he wants them to know how to dodge a bullet
and take out the enemy? What if he even wants them to win a battle when it looks like all odds are against them?

Hmmm, sounds a lot like the God of the Bible.

So what if God wants us to master the media and stop being
mastered by it?

Bottom line: it's up to us how much we personally take in. God
will speak to us, acting as a filter of what we should and shouldn't
funnel into our minds and our kids' minds. It's up to us to choose
to listen and obey or not.

Personally, I believe he's a great filter. When I listen to his voice,
I do well. When I ignore it, things get rocky and sometimes I crash,
hurting others and hurting myself.

Let's close this heavy-duty discussion with a funny story. During the writing of this book, I unplugged from all social media. Easy
for me. But then toward the last few weeks of writing, I declared a
fast from all screens except for this manuscript. I am so easily distracted that if I even open email, I might not write all day. So on the
final stretch, I refused email. I insisted I would look at nothing on a
screen but this book in your hands—which, to me, isn't a book. It's
a dream and an assignment.

I really tried to fast from the screens, but I couldn't fully do it.

Friends were texting me encouraging notes, and I felt like I had to respond—at least on the bathroom breaks! Next thing you know I'm passing notes with my friends via text, staring at another screen, committing adultery on my manuscript! Then I would get a text that said I had an important email; so I would open the inbox to read it and see all the unimportant ones. Suddenly I'm unsubscribing from stuff, clicking all these buttons that really don't matter. And I couldn't keep up with my kids' sports' schedules without constant email and calendar checking. I did my best—I really did—but it's almost impossible to completely get away from screens.

I was telling my hair stylist about my personal war with the screen, and she, who is never afraid to wield her authority, turned to my cell phone and pointed her finger at it.

"Be still!" she commanded. "You! Be still!"

We do need to tell the screens to be still sometimes, and to turn to our loved ones and see them and them only. We do need to stop the god of the immediate moment and invest long hours in something that will last. And we do need to stop being mastered by the media and become masterful over it.

We can use the media as a vehicle to get us where we need to go. Or we can use it as a vehicle to pick up someone else who may be lost and get them where they need to go.

10

The Fifth Truth:

You Are a Chosen Ambassador

"You are my witnesses," declares the LORD,
"and my servants whom I have chosen."

ISAIAH 43:10

God Speaks

The media comprises multiple forms of communication intended to reach the masses. Sounds like a great way to reach people with my love. You can write books about my love, you can sing songs about my love, you can make videos and write poems and share thoughts about my love. Through the screen, you now have the ability to spread the fragrance of my love farther and wider than any generation before you.

Perhaps I've done this on purpose, because I want my people not only to speak to their neighbor, but also to speak to people on the other side of the world.

Yet the Internet also opens up a window frame to the world, and the world's ways can openly funnel into you. Anything can be used for my glory or your shame; it's all in how you use it.

My people are working through the web to build water wells, feed the starving, and rescue my children from human trafficking—an abomination in my eyes. People who understand their dominion over the web are using it as a vehicle to rescue the lost and help the suffering. Through the screen, wise women teach others on marriage, help mothers raise their children right, and inspire each other to fight hard for the dreams I embedded in their hearts. Men offer teaching full of wisdom and hope for troubled marriages, money, ministry, and more.

Yet the despicable truth is that while one human uses a webcam to record a message of hope, another uses it to usher predators right into children's bedrooms. While one woman cries for the rescue of the sexually abused, another places her own body up for sale. One man offers free audio messages to help you unlock the love in your marriage while another pays the penalty of pornography, locking himself and his wife behind steel bars of pain.

Never before have women been up against so many images in their men's eyes. The woman in the kitchen—the one cooking dinner and caring for the children and sleeping next to her husband at night—should not have to compete with a two-dimensional screen.

The screen god is ruining men's view of women's beauty too. Many are bowing their desires to it as if I don't see how it's wrecking their lives and their wives.

When a man's fixation on the screen makes the wife in his own home look less desirable, less beautiful, less worthy of attention, and less captivating, then the screen needs to be tossed. I don't care how difficult it is. The warrior in him must slay the dragon devouring his own family; he must be willing to remove the screen or turn away from it. He must ask himself what he must do to save his house.

I did. I gave up my precious Son, the one by my side, the only one I had, to save you!

What will you give up to save your family? Zeal for your house should consume you.

In the world of the screen god anything goes, and that's not how things work with me. A man can use the Internet to inflict evil as quickly as he can order a book about my love. The screen god doesn't protect my children and never will. So it's up to you mothers and fathers. You must *teach them to wear a shield, to buckle truth, to wield their sword and helmet their minds. You must teach them when it's time to get up on their feet, step away from the screen, and go face-to-face with the people who matter.*

You must teach them to look up and away from the screen, to look to me for their reflection.

But first, you must look to me.

Look through my eyes. Look through my eyes at everything you see.

God, Good

Have you ever noticed how the lead news stories are almost always bad news? Car crashes, escaped criminals, domestic violence, disasters, lying politicians—there is *so* much bad news.

By nature, the news is adversarial and duplicitous. Always looking for the shocker, the controversy, the tragedy, the accusation, the deceit. It's not that we need to turn our eyes from it, necessarily. We just need to realize that the news media capitalizes on the negative— and the media can lie to us.

But God is not a liar. He is a truth-teller, a straight-shooter. He is not a God of confusion, and he is not a God who profits from the bad news.

He is the God of the Good News.

The angel said to the shepherds, "Do not be afraid. I bring you *good news* that will cause *great joy* for all the people" (Luke 2:10). And when Jesus stood up in the temple, he quoted the prophet Isaiah, saying, "God's Spirit is on me; he's chosen me to preach the Message of *good news* to the poor, sent me to announce pardon to prisoners and recovery of sight to the blind, to set the burdened and battered free, to announce, 'This is God's year to act!'" (Luke 4:18-19 MSG). God sent Jesus to bring "*messages of joy* instead of news of doom, a praising heart instead of a languid spirit" (Isaiah 61:3 MSG).

After Jesus was crucified, resurrected, and ascended to heaven, the political climate of Paul's culture was in upheaval. The religious world was wracked with turmoil and believers faced derision and execution. What did Paul tell them to do? Announce the bad news? Proclaim violence? Publish division?

No! He told them to preach the good news.

Lift up your eyes, he said. Fix them on the good. Meditate on what is "true, noble, reputable, authentic, compelling, gracious—the best, not the worst; the beautiful, not the ugly; things to praise, not things to curse" (Philippians 4:8 MSG).

Why did he tell them and us to focus on the life of Christ? To focus on the good? Because the more we focus on something the more we reflect it, and he wants us to "shine...like stars in the sky" as we hold out the word of life (Philippians 2:15). The world needs more goodness, more victory, more faith, more light, more healing, and more hope.

I wish the lead news were stories from ministries who are going straight into the heart of darkness—the brothels of Greece and Southeast Asia and other parts of the world—rescuing little girls and boys from sex trafficking. There are more slaves in the world today than at any point in human history: 27 million men, women, and children across the globe are in forced manual and sexual labor against their will. Ministries around the world are restoring whole communities with resources, education, medical care, safe houses, and job training. As one might rescue a child from a burning building, so heroes are rescuing little girls from forced sex slavery. [12]

That to me is good news; that is *headline* news. But mainstream media will not focus on it.

I wish even my local news would feature a ministry called "We Are Cherished" just down the street from me, where selfless women keep an open house with a hot dinner for strippers in the area. The women at We Are Cherished also march into the strip clubs on a regular basis and give the dancers gifts and an invitation to dinner.

When the dancers come to the Cherished House, volunteers lovingly outfit these women from the sex industry in beautiful clothes and help them get an education, leave their pimps, and start a new life in Christ. That's what I call beauty.[13]

My former student, who rose above cutting, suicidal thoughts, addiction, date rape, and bulimia, could be a great feature story. I can see it now: "A girl picks a better life! That's our lead story in tonight's news. And tonight at 11:00, two more girls set free in Cambodia! Freedom from strip clubs—good news from your own backyard!" Now that would be great. We could publish peace. We could proclaim salvation. We could focus on freedom.

To be fair, the news media does feature some good news, just not a lot of it, and the "good" and "bad" is totally subjective and filtered through the opinions of the network. What is good for one is not good for another: It's duplicitous.

But God does not have two faces. He has one face: Good.

There was a season in my life when I was so confused that I could not distinguish good from evil. I know that sounds nuts, but looking back on my life as a model and looking at the stormy season of my temple-clearing, I got seriously confused.

My counselor showed me this simple formula:

$$GOD = GOOD$$
$$DEVIL = EVIL$$

There is only one letter differing the spelling of *God* and *good* and one letter between *devil* and *evil*.

Our world calls evil good and good evil. But that couldn't be further from the truth. When something is good, it is God good. When something is evil, it is Evil Devil. It sounds simple, and it is. It helped me distinguish what was good in my life from what was not good; what was not healthy for me and what was. It also helped me develop boundaries around myself to protect my family.

I knew nothing about boundaries when I was a young woman. I understood morality, but not boundaries. "Above all else," Proverbs 4:23 says, "guard your heart, for everything you do flows from it." We are to be vigilant about protecting our hearts. Girls need to be taught that only good is allowed in. No evil. The moment something we see on the screen makes us feel invaluable is the moment we close the window. The moment someone compromises us online or otherwise is the moment they are not our "friend" anymore.

If we aren't wise, the media's values can sweep us away and we can forget what we are here for. We are not here to spend our lives chitter-chattering on social media for others' approval or allowing the screens to suck away our precious time. The truth is, there are people all over the world who need us to hold out our hands and reach for their miracles. The world is in need of people who understand their purpose and who use the media as a vehicle for good.

Chosen

We cannot become overwhelmed by the rampant evil of our world and shut down, assuming we are powerless to do anything about it. We are not powerless. Those of us who are in Christ have within us the power that raised him from the dead.

Christ was called "The Chosen One" (Luke 23:35). We always see who we are in the reflection of who he is. "I have chosen you out of the world," he said (John 15:19). Isaiah wrote, "You are my witnesses," declares the Lord, "and my servants whom I have chosen… From the east I summon a bird of prey; from a far-off land, a man to fulfill my purpose…I took you from the ends of the earth, from its farthest corners I called you. I said, 'You are my servant'; I have chosen you and not rejected you. So do not fear, for I am with you; do not be dismayed, for I am your God. I will strengthen you and help you; I will uphold you with my righteous right hand" (Isaiah 43:10, 46:11, 41:9-10).

He picked us to represent him not because we were great, but because we were weak, and in our weakness, he can be our strength. Paul calls us "Christ's ambassadors, as though God were making his appeal through us." An ambassador is a diplomatic official of the highest rank, representing the authority of the one who sent him. Serving his home country in a foreign land, the ambassador reflects and enforces the beliefs and practices of the one who sent him.

But here's the good news: It's not about our power; it's about the power of the Most High God living and acting through us. All we have to do is raise our hands and say, "Here I am, Lord! Send me!"

Where he sends us and how he sends us is up to him. No matter where we go, inside, we go on our knees. We go representing a good God. A high God. The Most High.

Go and Tell One Girl

The Bible is full of great ambassadors. Paul, who had once stood by approving the execution of Christians, became one of the greatest. "To live is Christ and to die is gain," he wrote in Philippians 1:21. Other ambassadors were regular people who followed a heavenly call. Our résumés do not prepare us for the life of the ambassador. Our histories do not declare our worthiness.

Christ in us is the only measure of our influence.

The first ambassador of the Good News, Mary Magdalene, was one messed-up lady. Jesus healed her of her demons and then made her the mouthpiece to announce his resurrection.

Mary Magdalene Speaks

Oh, how I adored him! He was the one my soul loved.
Before I met Jesus, I felt tortured. No one knew what was wrong with

me. *I certainly couldn't attract a man. I was sick, possessed by demons, which meant no one understood the source of my pain. "Demons" was a way to swipe their hand across my disease and say, "Well, the devil's got her by the throat."*

In many ways, seven to be exact, they were right. Disease, disorder, confusion, betrayal, sin, division, and angst were mine. They were my seven.

Then he came around the corner like a blazing light. I saw hope coming at me in an instant. I knew who he was, the one my soul cried for.

When Jesus healed me, it was one-on-one, just me and him in the woods of my wandering. When I heard his voice say, "Mary, you are healed," it was over. The suffering ceased. So what else could I do but follow his every step? I had no husband; no children. I followed him all the way from Galilee. The pain of watching him die was the worst agony of my life; he was all I had. He was the one my soul loved, and they stole him from me.

When everyone went home to obey the Sabbath, I came before dawn to the garden while it was still dark, but the stone was rolled away. I went inside, but he wasn't there.

"No!" I cried. "They have taken my Lord away and I don't know where they have put him!" My soul writhed.

"Woman, why are you crying? Who is it you are looking for?" I heard a voice behind me.

"Sir, if you have carried him away, tell me where you have put him, and I will go get him."

"Mary," he said, his tender voice in my ears a dove in the night.

At first I thought he was the gardener, but then I realized it was he. "Rabboni!" I cried, "Teacher!" I tried to cling to him.

But he backed up, warning me not to touch him, for he had not yet returned to the Father. He told me to go to the disciples and tell them the news—tell them that he had risen.

Every muscle in my body said to stay. I cannot leave you again, I thought—I want to be with you in the garden forever.

But I had to let go. I had to turn from what I could see to what I could not see. What I could see was temporary; what I could not see was eternal. So I ran.

"Mary, go and tell" were the sweetest words I ever heard.

Of course the disciples didn't believe crazy Mary. They had to go and see for themselves. But what they saw was true: He had risen. Then he appeared to them again and gave them the same message he first gave Mary: Go tell the good news.

Some legends say Mary went on to fast and pray in the wilderness, tortured by demons. Other legends say she went on to be a preacher on an island. I don't believe she disappeared into the wilderness endlessly. She had already been called out of the wilderness and given a purpose: She was a mouthpiece for the one her soul loved.

I'm sure the enemy tried to ruin her, but he couldn't.

Some ambassadors may get discouraged when they pour out their lives and only reach one girl. With sex trafficking, stripping, and prostitutes, it's one girl at a time. One girl called out of the darkness and passing into the light at a time. Some may feel like they are failing, only reaching one girl. But that's how God heals people: He speaks to the masses and he touches one soul. And through that one soul he speaks to the masses—and another soul is touched. It goes on and on, a little stone thrown into a big lake, and concentric circles echoing from that one stone.

I once gave my testimony at a women's Christmas banquet. The women had erected a massive white tent and filled it with tables, candles, and endless lights. That evening the tent was filled with almost romantic excitement. Waiting behind a curtain, I was on my knees. When I stood up, I was super energized and ready to get on the stage. I could feel my feet grow hot in my tall black boots, wanting to move up to the platform the moment I was called. I felt this fire in my soul and once the mike went on, it came out in my voice. That night, I could feel my Savior living inside of me as surely as I know he lives.

At the end of the talk, I asked if anyone wanted to accept him. As I offered the invitation, a dark, sweeping lull came over the room, like a hazy veil, and a sleepy stupor seemed to overcome the women. They all bowed their heads and kept them down.

"Who will believe?" I asked, the sound echoing in the massive tent.

Then, on the far side of the room, I saw one girl. She raised her hand high, reaching toward the ceiling. Then her whole body rose out of her seat, and she stretched her hand high and tall as she could, overextending it. She was the only one to receive Christ that blessed night.

From the stage, I saw a picture of the world—heads down, hearts closed, darkness like a veil resting over souls. And I saw the faith of one girl.

I was that girl once, in a world where the storm cloud hung low and it felt like nobody could see. I wanted God like I wanted life, and I found the one my soul loved.

Something happens when God gets ahold of one girl: He gets ahold of another girl, and another girl, and another. The next thing you know, we are shaking the earth with our faith, stomping our boots, freeing the captives.

The girl is never the same, and neither is the world around her.

Redeemed

My cheek is still pressed to the couch and I wouldn't open my eyes if I could. No way—I am still at the temple, and Jesus just winked at me from the center. It's so amazing that I am here, that I can see all the people praising him in unison. It feels so personal, like he is so excited to show me how great it all is. It is great. It feels like the fullness of joy.

Then suddenly the slideshow changes slides. Now I am back at the meadow where I started, inside a large wooden bunkhouse. There are lots and lots of bunks, and all my girlfriends are there. We are all hugging our pillows and snuggled up in our blankets, eagerly anticipating a bedtime story.

Jesus is sitting on the edge of a bunk, larger than life. He is holding a huge book. "The Book of Stories" is written on the spine.

"Would you like me to tell you a story?" he asks.

"Yes, Lord! Oh, yes!" we say, our voices in harmony.

Then he opens the giant book and reads us a story.

Next to how much I love him, I love the temple. And next to how much I love the temple, I love a sleepover. And next to how much I love a sleepover, I love a great story.

The slideshow changes slides.

It is morning. I am wrapped in a woolen blanket, sitting in a rocker on the deck of the bunkhouse, overlooking the meadow. Jesus brings me a piping hot cup of fresh coffee and sits down beside me.

The ranch is before us. The meadow is an endless field of wheat-colored grass and wispy flowers. Beyond it is the thicket of woods, and beyond that, the hills and mountains in the distance. I turn to smile, and there, right beside him, is Shane. Coffee in his hand, sitting in the rocker on the other side of Jesus.

Shane and Jesus start laughing and being silly together. As personal as the temple was for me, Jesus is equally as personal with Shane.

The slideshow changes slides.

Shane is now on Jesus's shoulders, and Jesus is larger than life, carrying him through the meadow to see the view. Shane thinks they are going to hunt, and has a rifle in his hand. But ever so gently, Jesus takes the rifle down and trades it for a telescope. They head into the thicket of woods. And then there is a deer—alive and completely tame. They go right up to it and Jesus shows Shane how he can stroke the velvet on its antlers.

As excited as he was to show me the temple, Jesus is thrilled to show Shane the deer.

The slideshow changes slides, and our whole family is walking through the meadow. The children are draped all over Shane's robust and redeemed frame. Behind them I follow, walking in peace and joy.

Circling our heels are our precious dogs, running and bounding in the field.

Everything is redeemed.

There was a time in my life when I felt like someone had swept my feet out from underneath me and I was broken in shards all over the ground. I felt like I should stop speaking, stop writing, and just be silent. I felt like I should just close up shop and be done. Life got so painful that I didn't think I could be a light anymore.

Then we went to church one day. The huge crowd of people were singing and praising and I was just crying. Glad when we could sit down, I sunk into the chair, my shoulders slumped forward.

Our ministry had just produced some special bracelets with the identity message on them. They had five symbols on them to remind you that you are God's daughter, creation, temple, light, and ambassador, with the feet fitted with the readiness of the good news.

I was wearing the bracelet for the first time that day. Feeling horrible, I was looking down at it, fiddling with the little charms.

No, I'm not, I thought. *I'm not a princess! I'm not a temple! I'm no ambassador. I'm not any of these things. I'm not!*

I didn't hear a word of what the pastor said. But then, I looked up. "Point One," he recited. Then these words came across the screen, one letter at a time:

Your identity is more powerful than your brokenness.

My faithful friend, you who have traveled far and wide and deep with me now, your identity is more powerful than your brokenness.

Don't ever stop believing. Don't ever stop speaking. By the word of our testimony and the blood of the Lamb, we shall overcome. You are more than a conqueror. He who is in you is greater than he who is in the world. Don't give up. Fight the good fight. Finish the race.

You are God's beloved daughter.

You are his precious creation.

You are his beautiful temple.

You are his shining light.

You are his chosen ambassador.

> Your eyes will see the king in his beauty and view a land that stretches afar (Isaiah 33:17).

Afterword:

P.S. Pass It On

My heart for this message is that you would pass it on. Too many women and girls are focused on the mirrors that lie. We have to turn their heads to the mirror that never changes. The younger generation needs our voices to rise high and strong above the tides of the culture.

We have to help them navigate the stormy world. Their identity is their rudder, and we have to teach them to keep their eyes fixed on the Son.

To him, we are all daughters, creations, temples, lights, and ambassadors. To him, we are all beautiful, and Truth living inside us makes us stunning.

Pass it on.

Notes

1. Carolyn Coker Ross, "Why Do Women Hate Their Bodies?" *World of Psychology* (blog), *Psych Central,* June 2, 2012, http://psychcentral.com/blog/archives/2012/06/02/why-do-women-hate-their-bodies/.

2. Nancy Etcoff et al., *The Real Truth About Beauty: A Global Report* (Dove Beauty Report, September 2004), 9.

3. Shuan Dreisbach, "Shocking Body-Image News: 97% of Women Will Be Cruel to Their Bodies Today," *Glamour,* March 2011, http://www.glamour.com/health-fitness/2011/02/shocking-body-image-news-97-percent-of-women-will-be-cruel-to-their-bodies-today.

4. Ibid.

5. Antoine de Saint Exupéry, *The Little Prince* (London: Wordsworth Editions Ltd., 1958), 82.

6. C.S. Lewis, *The Weight of Glory* (New York: HarperCollins, 2001), 42.

7. Edith Zimmerman, "99 Ways to Be Naughty in Kazakhstan: How Cosmo Conquered the World," *New York Times,* August 3, 2012.

8. Miriam Grossman, *Unprotected: A Campus Psychiatrist Reveals How Political Correctness in Her Profession Endangers Every Student* (New York: Penguin Group, 2007), xvii.

9. Ibid., xx

10. Ibid., xvii-xviii.

11. Ibid., 3

12. To find out how the A-21 Campaign and the Pearl Alliance are acting to abolish modern-day slavery and human trafficking, go to http://www.thea21campaign.org/ and http://messengerinternational.org/get-involved/pearl-alliance/.

13. To find out how We Are Cherished is helping women in Texas leave the sex industry, go to http://www.wearecherished.com/.

About the Author

Jennifer Strickland is wife to her best friend, Shane. Together they have three beautiful children, Olivia, Zachary, and Samuel. They live in North Texas, where they enjoy the Legacy8 family ranch. Their family's hope is also to build a restoration house where young women and girls can be healed. Their ministry, U R More, is devoted to restoring the beauty and value of women one girl at a time.

To learn more about Jennifer's
powerful resources and live events, go to
www.jenniferstrickland.net.

Beautiful Lies Study Guide
You Are More Than *What Men Think
*What the Mirror Reflects *What Magazines Tell You
JENNIFER STRICKLAND

Women who desire to go deeper in their study of culture's lies and how to overcome them can do so with the help of this growth and study guide. Building on the principles in Jennifer Strickland's book Beautiful Lies, individuals as well as small groups and Bible studies will discover...

- the truth of how deeply they are loved
- how to live out their radiant faith in a world consumed by darkness
- how to develop a true understanding of their identity and value

This workbook and Bible study is designed to be used along with Beautiful Lies.

To learn more about Harvest House books and
to read sample chapters, log on to our website:

www.harvesthousepublishers.com

HARVEST HOUSE PUBLISHERS
EUGENE, OREGON

BV 4527 .S744 2013
Strickland, Jennifer.
Beautiful lies

                              ,